LIFE SKILLS AND ADOLESCENT MENTAL HEALTH

Can school teach us to master life? This book confronts what the author sees as an ongoing trend in many Western democracies where citizens are increasingly being held accountable for their health and happiness.

The author believes that the introduction of life skills in school shows a tendency to place more responsibility on the individual rather than address fundamental societal flaws that really should be solved politically. It examines how such responsibility to psychologically deal with these problems affects our mental health and quality of life. This book questions the fundamentals of the life mastery curriculum where we might be risking the creation of just another arena where children have to perform, challenging readers to evaluate more closely the premises, consequences and limitations of life mastery.

The book, one of the first to question "life mastery" as an achievable goal with critical reviews of the 21st century skills movement, will be of interest to psychologists, school counsellors, teachers, students, politicians, and any reader evaluating school curriculums in relation to the decline in youth and adolescent mental health.

Ole Jacob Madsen is Professor of Cultural and Community Psychology at the University of Oslo, Norway. His previous works include: *The Therapeutic Turn* (2014), *Optimizing the Self* (2015), *The Psychologization of Society* (2018), *The Routledge International Handbook of Therapeutic Cultures* (2020) and *Deconstructing Scandinavia's "Achievement Generation"* (2021).

Routledge Focus on Mental Health

Routledge Focus on Mental Health presents short books on current topics, linking in with cutting-edge research and practice.

For a full list of titles in this series, please visit www.routledge.com/Routledge-Focus-on-Mental-Health/book-series/RFMH

Life Skills and Adolescent Mental Health

Can Kids Be Taught to Master Life?

Ole Jacob Madsen

Routledge
Taylor & Francis Group
LONDON AND NEW YORK

First English edition published 2023
by Routledge
4 Park Square, Milton Park, Abingdon, Oxon, OX14 4RN

and by Routledge
605 Third Avenue, New York, NY 10158

*Routledge is an imprint of the Taylor & Francis Group,
an informa business*

© 2024 Ole Jacob Madsen

First Norwegian edition published by Spartacus 2020

ISBN: 978-1-032-44512-0 (hbk)
ISBN: 978-1-032-44514-4 (pbk)
ISBN: 978-1-003-37254-7 (ebk)

DOI: 10.4324/9781003372547

Typeset in Times New Roman
by Apex CoVantage, LLC

Contents

Preface

Introduction

In the middle of August 2020, when the 636,000 Norwegian primary school pupils returned from their generous two-month summer holiday, something had ostensibly changed. The Norwegian Directorate for Education and Training had, as a part of its subject renewal policy decided that three transverse themes should now be taught through previously established subjects such as Norwegian, mathematics and gymnastics.[1] These three themes – health and life skills, sustainable development and democracy and citizenship – were highlighted to reflect current key societal issues that present-day youth would inevitably and necessarily face during their lifetime. However, of the three themes, I will limit myself to, and predominately examine, the objectives and unfolding and potential consequences/pitfalls of health and life skills (or, as it is more literally translated and is occasionally referred to by myself, "life mastery") in this book.

The main question I try to answer is: Why are health and life skills being introduced in public schools at this time? The least sensational reply might highlight that the school curriculum is just being updated to be of relevance to the societal changes and challenges of the 21st century. That is certainly a conceivable answer. However, an important motivation behind the examination in this book is the conviction that these changes in schools are also an expression of a deeper, and potentially troublesome, transformation in how we have come to think about individuals' wellbeing and mental health. Without giving too much away, behind the subject renewal policy is the idea that the upcoming generation needs guidance in how to live their lives and take responsible choices for their own health, and that it is up to the public schools to provide them with this. This may lead to the following questions: Has education not always provided youth with both knowledge and a basic set of skills such as reading, writing and calculating that prepares them for their life as grown-ups? Why is there suddenly an urge to highlight and address life skills as something explicit in itself?

International readers, unaccustomed to the public debate and concerns in Norway, might perhaps ask themselves whether something particularly worrisome is going on in this far-off, northern yet oil- and gas-blessed country that calls for this seemingly dramatic step. Yet the answer, I believe, is "no". The current changes in Norwegian public schools are an expression of a broader apprehension that is set to inevitably arise, or has already taken place, in most countries globally – although not necessarily always operationalised through the teaching of health and life skills. The tendency I am referring to is an outspoken concern for adolescents' mental health. A possible solution to this uneasiness is to use psychoeducation and teach children healthy coping strategies for handling stress and pressure in a way that prevents them turning into anxiety, depression, self-harm or eating disorders. Moreover, a potential place to do that is in public schools, since these are institutions where almost all children and adolescents will spend a large share of their day throughout their formative years. Norway may well be one of the first countries that explicitly introduces health and life skills as a subject for all pupils – although indirectly through the established body of teaching. However, in many Western countries, as I will show henceforth, there are examples of a similar tendency in the last couple of years. All of these programs, globally, are faced with some of the same dilemmas presented in this book. My aim – and hope – is that my critical examination of the introduction of health and life skills in Norwegian schools can also serve as a useful scrutinisation of the potential pitfalls elsewhere, whether similar life skills programs have already been introduced or governments or professionals are seriously considering them. I also hope that it serves not only as an examination of life skills in schools but also of wider questions about the role of education and ultimately how much responsibility one could reasonably ask young people to take for their own mental health.

The case of Sweden

One does not have to go far from Norway's borders to find a similar line of thought. In fact, in the winter of 2022, several organisations, including UNICEF, Save the Children and Bris, came together in Sweden to make a public call for mental health education to be made compulsory in schools. Their request that the Swedish National Agency for Education put mental health on the curriculum is fascinatingly similar to the calls made by organisations in Norway years prior to this. The following is a transcript of an entire news story from Radio Sweden.

> Children should learn about mental health in schools just like they learn about physical health, that's according to 16 organizations who work with children's wellbeing and health in Sweden. Karin Schulz from the organization Mind: "We see several warning signs. Many children say they are mentally unwell and they turn to the health service more than ever before because of mental illness. And the

prescription of anti-depressants are increasing a lot", she says. "So that is why we think it is important to think preventatively to equip children and young people with knowledge and tools so that they can understand themselves and their surroundings better", she says. The organizations including UNICEF, Save the Children and Bris want to make mental health education compulsory for all students in primary as well as secondary school. In an op-ed piece in the daily Dagens Nyheter, they claim every other 15 year old today is suffering from mental health problems, which is twice as many in the beginning of the 1980s. They say that the results from the research are clear: young people that learn about mental health feel better. They learn how to take care of their mental health. As well as where they can turn for help if they need it. The organizations refer to Finland, New Zealand and some states in the US where mental health already is on the curriculum and say it is time for Sweden to put it there too. But it is up to the national agency for education to decide whether to make it a subject in its own right or integrate it into the current PE-classes, says Karin Schulz from Mind. "We don't say exactly how this should be done, but we think it is vital knowledge that all children have the right to", she says. In addition to the classes to teach children about mental health the organization also wants to include it in the regular health checks that children undergo at school.[2]

What is both intriguing and potentially worrisome is that this line of thinking is almost identical to that of Norway a few years earlier. The parallel basic assumption appears to be that there are perturbing signs of a mental health epidemic among younger people in our country. Therefore, something must be done. That "something" is prevention in schools by giving children more knowledge and tools so that they can "understand themselves and their surroundings better". To support this, there is the disputable claim that research allegedly shows that young people who learn about mental health feel and fare better. The only uncertainty is connected to how this should be rolled out in schools in practice. For instance, whether it should be an independent subject in its own right or integrated into the current PE classes.

An optimistic interpretation would be that these calls for education in life skills and mental health in both Norwegian and Swedish schools are similar only because the problem of youths' declining mental health is alike in most countries; the necessity of teaching children life skills and educating them about mental health in public schools appears to have gained momentum in several countries worldwide. Yet, a more sceptical view – to which I will subscribe in fair shares in this book – is that organisations and governments around the world are, by default, drawn to the simplest and most readily available "package" and individual "solution" to societal problems that does not require institutional changes.

Look to Finland

If we move even further east to Finland, which Schulz advised Swedish educators to do, what do we find there? Initially, it is worth stating that Finland's educational system is frequently ranked as the best in the world. Often the practice of delaying the start of education to age seven, fewer mandatory standardised tests, a low amount of homework and the unique prestige teachers hold are mentioned. However, a recent report in *The Lancet Child & Adolescent Health* journal pointed to a perhaps overlooked component: Social and health care for students provided by the schools themselves.[3] After the introduction of legislation in 2014, it became a requirement that school staff paid attention to their students' wellbeing and welfare. Teachers were also encouraged to take any concerns about their students – if they were given permission – to one or all members of the schools health and welfare team. This was also backed up by a seven-day time limit for appointments after a concern was raised, and just one day if the situation was judged as critical. Moreover, the school nurse routinely meets all pupils individually each year, and a doctor on specific years. Furthermore, health education is also introduced as a special subject for students from the 7th grade onwards. Typically, focus points will be bullying, diet, prevention of illness, good health and safety and mental health – the latter allegedly given extended attention to keep it from being stigmatised.

Now, this sounds almost too good to be true. Yet current development in Finland is not without its alarms for the future either. In the aforementioned report, Silja Kosola, who has worked as a Helsinki-based school doctor for 8 years, acknowledges the benefits of her home country's health and welfare system for children but is also open about her concerns for the direction they are currently taking, mentioning both the dangers of over-screening and medicalisation.[4] For instance, the juxtaposition of school nurses being routinely advised to screen for depression among 15-year-olds using the Beck Depression Inventory and their inevitably finding more teenagers with mild to moderate symptoms. A consequence of this might be that the child psychiatric services are over-stretched; and that those with more resourceful parents get help over those with less privileged backgrounds but often more severe problems. In the interview, Kosola therefore also ponders on whether such broad-scale assessments and interventions form the most beneficial approach, or whether the resources could ideally be used better if they were deployed more selectively.[5] Whether the investment in social and mental health will be successful remains to be seen. Finland has had some success in reducing externalised symptoms in recent decades, not least suicide, yet internalised symptoms, such as depression, anxiety, stress and self-esteem issues, have increased in later years – particularly among girls – a pattern all too familiar for most Western countries.[6]

Something is rotten in the state of Denmark

If we move further south to Denmark, the government decided in 2018 to form a National Stress Panel, given the background of a worrying increase in self-reported levels of stress among Danish youth throughout the 2010s. One year later, this commission presented twelve actions meant to reverse this negative trend.[7] Their third specific plan of action was to prepare children and adolescents to master life better, and their suggestion was that life skills should be established as a recurrent theme in Danish public schools, modelled on the recently decided changes in Norway. This proposed plan of action was welcomed by the leader of the students' organisation, Sarah Gruszow Bærentzen, but simultaneously dismissed by the leader of the teacher's union, Anders Bondo Christensen, and the minister of Education, Merete Riisager from the Liberal Alliance – whose main reaction was that it was not a school's mandate to solve societal problems.[8] In a previous interview, Riisager also argued that the main problem was not a culture of achievement in education based on tests, presentations and grades but a culture of perfection, which transcends life in school and hangs over youths' heads in all walks of life.[9] Not only that, Riisager appears to interpret suggestions like teaching life skills in schools as an expression of disclaiming liability by her generation of adults. That this ultimately hurts the children, who themselves are forced to behave as adults, is the underlying message. Despite Riisager's initial success in rejecting the incorporation of life skills in schools in Denmark, the debate of what to do about the growing discontent, stress and mental health complaints among Danish youth continues with increased intensity. For instance, the Danish Socialist Party have youth discontent as their top political priority. However, their remedy is directed more at relieving the pressure in the education system, a more practical curriculum and the presence of more adults in classes and schools.[10] It is also worth mentioning that despite there not being a national curriculum in health and life skills, Danish municipalities are still recommended to follow the philosophy of early intervention and implement established programs, such as PALS ("Positive behaviour, supportive learning environment and interaction in school") and ABC ("Act Belong Commit") in schools. Many municipalities have done just that.[11] Meanwhile, the worry about young people's declining mental health appears to increase each year in Denmark, as reflected during the Danish Election in 2022, when this issue became one of the major topics in the debates prior to the election of a new government.

Back in the UK

In the UK, "Personal, social and emotional development" has become one of three prime areas within the Early Years Foundation Stage, a statutory framework introduced in the British government's Childcare Act in 2006. Self-regulation, managing the self, building relationships and understanding your feelings are some of the key components here. Ideally, the typical student should "show an understanding of their own feelings and those of others, and begin to regulate their behaviour accordingly".[12] Back in 2008, Kathryn Ecclestone and Dennis Hayes published their seminal book *The Dangerous Rise of Therapeutic Education* that aimed to explain why Western society has seemingly come to regard today's youth as less psychologically resilient than their predecessors. As an illustration, they began their book with a memorable quote from a history teacher in London: "[y]ou know something has changed when young people want to know more about themselves than about the world".[13] The English education system had in recent decades, according to Ecclestone and Hayes, been permeated by psycho-emotional practices, programs and rhetoric, which suggested that the primary trait of education was no longer that of knowledge but rather of safety and personal development. In the reprint of their book from 2019 the new preface is entitled "The continuing dangerous rise of therapeutic education", which suggests that the trends they noted in the early 21st century have only increased since.[14] State support for psychological, social and emotional learning is immense across most political parties. For example, the Labour government's Social and Emotional Aspects of Learning (2003–2010) was heavily influenced by positive psychology, person-centred counselling and cognitive behavioural therapy (CBT), and the Liberal Democrat/Conservative coalition that the following year replaced "emotional wellbeing" with "character" and "resilience" – perhaps more in line with their ideological values but still in line with the same thinking. Currently popular interventions in primary schools, such as mindfulness, have seen the Welfare Trust spending £6.4 million to explore the benefits of mindfulness classes in schools. Notwithstanding, young people's mental health problems appear only to worsen in the UK. One in six children aged between 5 and 16 was believed to have a mental health problem in 2021, whereas that number was one in nine four years prior to that.[15] It should be mentioned that, of course, the Covid-19 pandemic (as in most countries) is believed to be partly responsible for this negative trend due to increased isolation and loneliness among young people, the negative consequences of which might be reversed as society gradually re-opens.

Life skills around the world

My earlier suggestion that there are suspicious similarities across borders in the line of thought that life skills and mental health should be taught in schools may have a reasonable explanation. Life skills has been on the agendas of global and influential organisations like the World Health Organization (WHO), which are defined as more or less universal, for the past decades. As far back as 1977, the WHO highlighted the necessity of promoting health as a positive concept and resource for everyday life. This was later agreed in the Ottawa Charter for Health Promotion in 1986. Following up on this, the WHO issued the seminal report "Life Skills Education for Children and Adolescents in Schools" in 1994. In the opening paragraphs, readers around the world can read the following:

> Promoting Psychosocial Competence: Psychosocial competence is a person's ability to deal effectively with the demands and challenges of everyday life. It is a person's ability to maintain a state of mental well-being and to demonstrate this in adaptive and positive behaviour while interacting with others, his/her culture and environment. Psychosocial competence has an important role to play in the promotion of health in its broadest sense; in terms of physical, mental and social well-being. In particular, where health problems are related to behaviour, and where the behaviour is related to an inability to deal effectively with stresses and pressures in life, the enhancement of psychosocial competence could make an important contribution. This is especially important for health promotion at a time when behaviour is more and more implicated as the source of health problems. The most direct interventions for the promotion of psychosocial competence are those which enhance the person's coping resources, and personal and social competencies. In school-based programmes for children and adolescents, this can be done by the teaching of life skills in a supportive learning environment.[16]

Here we find the whole idea of life skills in schools spelled out. Human behaviour is depicted as the major source of health problems, and now more than ever. However, although it may sound fairly straightforward, what is this notion really an expression of? One interpretation could simply lead to the perception that research has demonstrated that individual behaviour, or rather bad behaviour, is the single most important explanatory factor and predictor for health problems. Well, yes, but what does this really imply beyond the merely obvious? One implicit idea underlying this conception might be that, in the middle of the 1990s, most people in most Western countries no longer suffered from some of the social ills that previous generations did before them. Therefore, objectively, they could be held more accountable for their behaviour, either good or bad, than has traditionally been the case. Another possible interpretation, however, rejects this notion that all men are equal, and stresses that each individual's capability for displaying health-promoting behaviour and making sound and healthy choices for themself is still very much a result of where in the social pecking order you find yourself; whether you come from a family with plenty sociocultural resources, etc. In fact, if this latter explanation holds some truth to it, claiming that behaviour is the major source of health problems might actually help to disclose this fact, leaving the impression that those who succeed prosper because they have earned it. Notwithstanding, in fact, the whole game is "rigged" and life chances are extremely unfair in terms of where one starts in life.

Nonetheless, the WHO went on to list the following areas of life skills as vital across cultures: Decision-making and problem-solving, creative thinking, critical thinking, communication and interpersonal skills, self-awareness and empathy, assertiveness and equanimity, resilience and coping with emotions and coping with stress.[17] Perhaps also influenced by the positive psychology movement in recent years, life skills education is therefore frequently seen as supporting positive youth development, and something that prevents both delinquent behaviour and mental health problems:

> life skills education, have found [sic] to be an effective psychosocial intervention strategy for promoting positive social and mental health of adolescents, which plays an important role in all aspects such as strengthening coping strategies and developing self-confidence and emotional intelligence.[18]

In addition, it appears that life skills training is also understood to be increasingly important, perhaps as the upcoming generation's worry that the burden of societal challenges – and at the same time, the huge amount of stimuli and information they are exposed to on a daily basis in their digital lives – grows larger every day. According to the WHO, to date, life skills have often been taken for granted but are becoming more and more of a necessity:

> [T]here is growing recognition that with changes in many cultures and lifestyles, many young people are not sufficiently equipped with life skills to help them deal with the increased demands and stresses they experience. They seem to lack the support required to acquire and reinforce life skills. It may be that traditional mechanisms for passing on life skills (e.g. family and cultural factors) are no longer adequate considering the influences that shape young people's development. These include media influence and the effects of growing up in situations of cultural and ethnic diversity. Also the rapid rate of social change, witnessed in many countries, makes the lives of young people, their expectations, values, and opportunities very different from that of their parents.[19]

It appears that life skills are frequently perceived as the answer to the difficulty of being a young person that struggles or suffers from mental health issues at the beginning of the 21st century. More or less systematic attempts at life skills education can, in addition to the countries already mentioned, be found in Holland, Germany, Greece, Canada, the US, Mexico, Brazil, South Africa, Hong Kong, Pakistan, Nepal and India. Life skills also recurrently appear in worldwide development programmes that aim to empower young people, and girls in particular. However, they may produce contradictory outcomes when it comes to gender oppression. For instance, in Rajasthan, India, the life skills programme seeks to teach girls about bodily integrity but may, at the same time, accidently re-inscribe the caste norms.[20]

The universalised approach to skills in life is also frequently depicted as a kind of competency, where health is frequently depicted as a literacy on the same line as reading and writing:

> The underlying cause of the problem of confusion for many people is a low level of health literacy. Literacy skills in general are the strongest predictor of an individual's health status, more so than their income, age, education level or employment status.[21]

It is worth highlighting how having "health literacy" in many states globally is upheld as a personal responsibility and key to being an accountable citizen. Thankfully, it is still acknowledged that some groups may be disadvantaged and have difficulties in managing this demand. Yet the rhetoric then often narrows down to how governmental authorities should make sure that they equip these disadvantaged people with the necessary skills so that they can also become healthy citizens:

> Above all, health literacy should be, and needs to be, an active part of a person's citizenship and it is a key component of social inclusion. We should all take it upon ourselves to ensure we are as health literate as we possibly can be and make use of the courses and opportunities that are on offer. However, governments and other authorities have a critical role to play too – particularly for disadvantaged groups. At a time when most countries are investing in a number of initiatives for senior citizens, such as enhancing their computer skills, they also need to make sure that people are equally equipped to make healthy choices in supermarkets, restaurants, or when talking with their physicians. This will help safeguard the health of citizens into the future.[22]

However, it seems that the notion of health literacy started with research on the connection between low literacy skills (with regard to reading and writing) and poor health among medical patients.[23] Gradually this finding appears to evolve and lead to talk about "health literacy" as a competency in itself; rather than just an expression of patients with low levels of education and wealth who also have poorer health than peers from more privileged backgrounds.[24] Just as governments in the past – and in some cases in the present – around the world have had the prevention of illiteracy as one of their major goals, decision and policy makers around the world now need to react to their respective national concerns for their youth's mental health literacy and life competence.

Unsurprisingly, commercial companies that offer to follow up on this for governments and educational bodies regularly appear. These companies make convincing claims, quoting both science and bodies like the WHO. Just listen to how a typical representative of the education company Positive Action convincingly maintains their argument in 'Why Should We Be Teaching Life Skills in Schools in 2022?':

> The internet is a wildly useful innovation. Information has become faster, better and easier to attain – more so every year. Discover why kids and young adults need real-life skills empowerment now more than ever.
>
> However, because the information accessed via the internet is unfiltered, this has opened up a complex information age with a wide range of stimuli. It can get young people into an emotional mess.
>
> Not to mention the misinformation, cyberbullying, and other negative consequences affecting kids in the modern age – it's hard to cope.
>
> That's why kids and young adults need real-life skills empowerment, now more than ever. . .
>
> All-encompassing skills like these can't be left to learn in the home setting alone – especially since kids often spend more time in school.
>
> Imagine young people graduating from school with excellent scores but not knowing the first thing about coping with reality. What if they couldn't communicate effectively? Or couldn't handle money issues and were always in debt?
>
> It's both alarming and all-too-common. That's why parents and teachers alike should play an active role in preparing kids for the future.
>
> Where the school is concerned, that means doing more than merely teaching algebra and biology. While no one can downplay the importance of good academics, it's just not enough without the necessary life skills. . . . Setting Young People up for Success: Young people are brimming with untapped potential. And they need dedicated skills that empower them to bring out the best in themselves. . . . It's a proven philosophy. Get in touch with Positive Action today for the curriculum and kits, training, and more. Positive Action will help you achieve the best outcomes – well rounded, empowered, and educated young people.[25]

As is often said, something must be done – but not something too original (or costly)! So why *not* teach life skills in schools? Expressing hesitation is rapidly seen as somewhat *passe*, as the enthusiasts depict life skills as a new landmark discovery that is set to become a necessity. For example, Dan Domenech, the executive director of the US national School Superintendents Association, has said "[w]e are finally beginning to recognize that school is more than just teaching the kidsreading, writing and arithmetic."[26]

Conclusion

Teaching life skills is rapidly becoming the answer to a troublesome development among adolescents around the world. Yet, as I hope to show in this book, fundamental questions remain about whether life skills education really can fulfil its promises. There are both practical and pedagogical issues regarding whether it is the role of public schools and kindergartens to teach children and adolescents how to handle life, and whether they have the right resources and professional training to do this. Furthermore, there is a more universal existential dimension to this. The assumption and temptation to believe that life skills can be mastered so that children do not develop troublesome levels of anxiety, depression and stress, appear quite similar and touch upon many of the same dilemmas: Namely, how we as a society view and handle mental health and human suffering, in particular among young people. Moreover, the concept of life skills is also a question of ideology and political values, and how much individual responsibility for their life outcomes and mental health should be put on the shoulders of children and young people. Regardless of these reservations, the teaching of life skills is currently a popular solution that governments around the world recurrently appear to either test or seriously consider. Consequently, even if life skills or health literacy can actually be taught and mastered, this initiative is of such importance and impact that it deserves a larger contextualization than the enthusiastic supporters and organisations currently reflect. I therefore hope that by reading this book the reader will feel a little more enlightened, and able to consider and problematise whether we can, or should, teach children to master life in all its dimensions.

Notes

1 The Norwegian Directorate for Education and Training, "Fagfornyelsen [The subject renewal]" (2017), www.udir.no/laring-og-trivsel/lareplanverket/fagfornyelsen/.
2 Anders Jelmin, "Calls for mental health to be on the school curriculum", *Radio Sweden* (2022), https://sverigesradio.se/artikel/calls-for-mental-health-to-be-on-the-school-curriculum.
3 Cassandra Coburn, "Mental health in Finnish schools: So close to perfection", *The Lancet Child & Adolescent Health* 3, no. 12 (2019).
4 Ibid.
5 Ibid.
6 N. Knaappila, M. Marttunen, S. Fröjd, and R. Kaltiala, "Changes over time in mental health symptoms among adolescents in Tampere, Finland", *Scandinavian Journal of Child and Adolescent Psychiatry and Psychology* 9 (2021).
7 The Stress Panel, "Sammen kan vi knække stresskurverne [Together we can break the stress curves]" (The Ministry of Health and Ageing, 2019).
8 Emma Bæksgaard Christensen, "Stresspanelet vil lære unge at mestre livet [The stress panel wants to teach youths how to master life]", *Skolemonitor* (2019), https://skolemonitor.dk/nyheder/art7071979/Stresspanelet-vil-l%C3%A6re-unge-at-mestre-livet.
9 Tyson W. Lyall, "Vi har ingen præstationskultur. Vi har en perfekthedskultur, og det er meget værre ["We don't have an achievement culture: We have a perfectionist culture, and that is much worse]", *Altinget* (2018), www.altinget.dk/artikel/169809-vi-har-ingen-praestationskultur-vi-har-en-perfekthedskultur-og-det-er-meget-vaerre.
10 The Green Left, "Børn og unges mistrivsel skal øverst på dagsordenen [Children and youths discontent must be on top of the agenda]" (2023), https://sf.dk/maerkesager/mistrivsel-skal-oeverst-paa-dagsordenen/.

11 Danish Health Authority, "Børn og unges sundhed og trivsel [Children and adolescents health and wellbeing]" (Danish Health Authority, 2019).
12 Surrey County Council, "Personal social and emotional development in the eyfs" (2022), www.surreycc.gov.uk/schools-and-learning/childcare-professionals/early-years-foundation-stage/personal-social-and-emotional-development., par. 6.
13 Kathryn Ecclestone and Dennis Hayes, *The Dangerous Rise of Therapeutic Education* (London: Routledge, 2008), viii.
14 *The Dangerous Rise of Therapeutic Education*, Classic Edition Series ed. (London: Routledge, 2019).
15 Young Minds, "Mental health statistics" (2023), www.youngminds.org.uk/about-us/media-centre/mental-health-statistics/.
16 Health World Health Organization: Division of Mental, "Life skills education for children and adolescents in schools. Pt. 1: Introduction to life skills for psychosocial competence. Pt. 2: Guidelines to facilitate the development and implementation of life skills programmes" (Geneva: World Health Organization, 1994), 1.
17 Ibid.
18 R. Prajapati, B. Sharma, and D. Sharma, "Significance of life skills education", *Contemporary Issues in Education Research (CIER)* 10, no. 1 (2016): 4.
19 World Health Organization. Division of Mental, "Life skills education for children and adolescents in schools. Pt. 1: Introduction to life skills for psychosocial competence. Pt. 2: Guidelines to facilitate the development and implementation of life skills programmes", 5.
20 Aditi Arur and Joan DeJaeghere, "Decolonizing life skills education for girls in Brahmanical India: A dalitbahujan perspective", *Gender and Education* 31, no. 4 (2019).
21 Rick Kellerman and Barry D. Weiss, "Health literacy and the jama patient page", *JAMA* 282, no. 6 (1999).
22 Ilona Kickbusch, "Health literacy: An essential skill for the twenty-first century", *Health Education* 108, no. 2 (2008).
23 Kellerman and Weiss, "Health literacy and the jama patient page."
24 Kickbusch, "Health literacy: An essential skill for the twenty-first century."
25 Positive Action, "Why should we be teaching life skills in schools in 2022?", *Positive Action* (2021), www.positiveaction.net/blog/teaching-life-skills-in-schools.
26 Jocelyn Gecker and Dylan Lovan, "Youth mental health is in crisis: Are schools doing enough?", *AP News* (2022), https://apnews.com/article/mental-health-crisis-schools-768fed6a4e71d694ec0694c627d8fdca., par. 14.

References

Arur, Aditi and Joan DeJaeghere. "Decolonizing life skills education for girls in Brahmanical India: A Dalitbahujan perspective." *Gender and Education* 31, no. 4 (2019, 19.5.): 490–507.

Christensen, Emma Bæksgaard. "Stresspanelet vil lære unge at mestre livet [The stress panel wants to teach youths how to master life]." *Skolemonitor* (2019). Published electronically 6.3. https://skolemonitor.dk/nyheder/art7071979/Stresspanelet-vil-l%C3%A6re-unge-at-mestre-livet.

Coburn, Cassandra. "Mental health in Finnish schools: So close to perfection." *The Lancet Child & Adolescent Health* 3, no. 12 (2019, 12.1): 848–9.

Danish Health Authority. *Børn og unges sundhed og trivsel [Children and Adolescents Health and Wellbeing]*. Copenhagen: Danish Health Authority, 2019.

Ecclestone, Kathryn and Dennis Hayes. *The Dangerous Rise of Therapeutic Education*. London: Routledge, 2008.

———. *The Dangerous Rise of Therapeutic Education*. Classic Edition Series ed. London: Routledge, 2019.

Gecker, Jocelyn and Dylan Lovan. "Youth mental health is in crisis. Are schools doing enough?" *AP News* (2022). Published electronically 17.8. https://apnews.com/article/mental-health-crisis-schools-768fed6a4e71d694ec0694c627d8fdca.

The Green Left. "Børn og unges mistrivsel skal øverst på dagsordenen [Children and youths discontent must be on top of the agenda]." (2023). Published electronically 4.1. https://sf.dk/maerkesager/mistrivsel-skal-oeverst-paa-dagsordenen/.

Jelmin, Anders. "Calls for mental health to be on the school curriculum." *Radio Sweden* (2022). Published electronically 22.2. https://sverigesradio.se/artikel/calls-for-mental-health-to-be-on-the-school-curriculum.

Kellerman, Rick and Barry D. Weiss. "Health literacy and the Jama patient page." *JAMA* 282, no. 6 (1999): 525–7.

Kickbusch, Ilona. "Health literacy: An essential skill for the twenty-first century." *Health Education* 108, no. 2 (2008): 101–4.

Knaappila, N., M. Marttunen, S. Fröjd and R. Kaltiala. "Changes over time in mental health symptoms among adolescents in Tampere, Finland." *Scandinavian Journal of Child and Adolescent Psychiatry and Psychology* 9 (2021): 96–104.

Lyall, Tyson W. "Vi har ingen præstationskultur. Vi har en perfekthedskultur, Og det er meget værre [We don't have an achievement culture: We have a perfectionist culture, and that is much worse]." *Altinget* (2018). Published electronically 20.6. www.altinget.dk/artikel/169809-vi-har-ingen-praestationskultur-vi-har-en-perfekthed-skultur-og-det-er-meget-vaerre.

The Norwegian Directorate for Education and Training. "*Fagfornyelsen* [The subject renewal]." (2017). Published electronically 5.5. www.udir.no/laring-og-trivsel/lareplanverket/fagfornyelsen/.

Positive Action. "Why should we be teaching life skills in schools in 2022?" *Positive Action* (2021). Published electronically 28.1. www.positiveaction.net/blog/teaching-life-skills-in-schools.

Prajapati, R., B. Sharma and D. Sharma. "Significance of life skills education." *Contemporary Issues in Education Research (CIER)* 10, no. 1 (2016): 1–6.

The Stress Panel. *Sammen kan vi knække stresskurvene [Together We Can Break the Stress Curves]*. Copenhagen: The Ministry of Health and Ageing, 2019.

Surrey County Council. "Personal social and emotional development in the Eyfs." (2022). Published electronically 31.10. www.surreycc.gov.uk/schools-and-learning/childcare-professionals/early-years-foundation-stage/personal-social-and-emotional-development.

World Health Organization, Division of Mental Health. *Life Skills Education for Children and Adolescents in Schools. Pt. 1, Introduction to Life Skills for Psychosocial Competence. Pt. 2, Guidelines to Facilitate the Development and Implementation of Life Skills Programmes*. Geneva: World Health Organization, 1994.

Young Minds. "Mental health statistics." (2023). Published electronically 4.1. www.youngminds.org.uk/about-us/media-centre/mental-health-statistics/.

1   Life mastery

A user handbook

Life mastery. Savour the words. Who doesn't want to master life? And who would disagree that young people of today, in particular those experience so much stress and pressure, might benefit from learning life skills? Where better to start than in primary school and lower secondary schools that are attended by 99.88 per cent of all Norwegian children? Raising doubts about mental health and the life mastery skills that are now being introduced in Norwegian schools may appear to be a little mistrustful. But that is precisely the aim of this book. I would also argue that it is extremely important, as life mastery is an appealing concept that we perceive as something that "everyone" is in favour of. However, life skills are far from being as uncomplicated, side-effect-free and politically neutral as they may appear at first glance. It is likely, however, that the arguments in favour of life mastery probably need a little boost.

   The decision to introduce health and life skills in the schools as of autumn 2020 as an interdisciplinary subject raises a number of questions of both a principled and practical nature, from the very fundamental question of whether life can be mastered at all, and encompassing whether mastery is a good measure of our allotted time here on earth, to whether life mastery answers the particular challenges that young people in Norway grapple with, in addition to the more practical educational questions, such as whether life is masterable, and if so, can such mastery necessarily be taught? And if it can be taught, is it actually the school's job to teach it? Given that life mastery is a good standard for life and the right social medicine, that it can be taught and is the task of the school, do Norwegian teachers have the right skill set to teach the subject? If the answer to all this is "yes", there are still other important questions to answer: Can all students learn to mastery skills regardless of their start in life? If so, do students have a greater responsibility to master life than earlier? And if only some not all students take advantage of life mastery in school, then what about the rest?

   Even if the answers to these questions should only confirm the necessity for introducing life skills in schools, I believe they are nevertheless worth asking. While all objections may not necessarily be able to be addressed here,

DOI: 10.4324/9781003372547-1

the questions nevertheless provide an opportunity to look more closely at the premises, consequences and limitations of life mastery, which very rapidly has gone from being an unknown to becoming an integral part of the renewed Knowledge Promotion Reform that is aimed at making children and adolescents better able to meet the challenges of the future.

What is life mastery?

What does the much-hyped life mastery project mean in specific terms? It is not easy to answer without further ado, even though the concept has never been as important as it is now. Under the section on purpose in the Norwegian Education Act, Section 1–1 and in the curriculum for the Knowledge Promotion Reform in primary and lower secondary schools, the following is stated: "Students and apprentices will develop knowledge, competence and attitudes in order to be able to carve out their lives and be able to participate in work and community in society".[1] The official definition, which is part of a more extensive interpretation under which the Norwegian Directorate for Education and Training operates in connection with the Subject Renewal 2020, reads as follows:

Health and life skills as an interdisciplinary subject in schools will provide students with competence that promotes good mental and physical health and that provides opportunities to make responsible life choices. In childhood and adolescence, the development of a positive self-image and a confident identity are especially crucial.

A society that facilitates good health choices for the individual is of great importance to health. Life mastery is about being able to understand and being able to influence factors that impact the command of your own life. The subject will help students learn to deal with success and adversity and personal and practical challenges in the best possible way.

Current areas within the subject are physical and mental health, living habits, sexuality and gender, drugs, media use and consumption and personal finances. Value choices and the meaning of the meaning of life, interpersonal relationships, being able to set boundaries and respect the boundaries of others and be able to manage thoughts, emotions and relationships also belong under this subject.[2]

As presented here, life mastery sounds both appealing and comprehensive: From the meaning of – or rather in life – to being able to pay one's bills. It is probably also not coincidental that the sentence in the second paragraph, which most closely aspires to present a classic definition – "Life mastery is about being able to understand and being able to influence factors that impact the command of your own life" – is somewhat circular and quite vague in terms of actual content. Most teachers, parents or students who read this attempt at circumscribing from an official standpoint will probably still be left with a large number of unanswered questions about what life mastery actually is.

However, if we put our lives on hold for the time being, mastery (*coping*) is far more familiar and integrated in subjects such as psychology and public health work. Professor of Psychology Frode Svartdal's definition of coping is taken from *Store norske leksikon* and reads as follows:

> Coping is a widely used term in modern psychology that generally refers to the fact that a person handles tasks and challenges that are encountered throughout the course of life. It can involve specific tasks that require competence and skills (for example, pass an exam) or more comprehensive challenges (dealing with divorce, serious illness, persistent stress).[3]

Here we undoubtedly have answers to some of the earlier ambiguities, because the way coping is defined by Svartdal makes it primarily a collective term that refers to a series of different tasks and challenges that an individual encounters in life and is able to handle more or less adequately. Life mastery in school, on the other hand, can easily seem like a standalone universal skill that can be learnt through teaching and that fully equips one for later life. However, it is highly uncertain that life mastery understood in this way as a universal skill set, exists at all. Most of all, it appears to be a newly introduced construct.

Svartdal provides many examples of coping, including resilience, or psychological resilience, related in particular to challenges and crises in which an individual's optimism, self-esteem, courage, belief in their own ability and social support have a positive effect, while negative thinking and rumination have a negative impact on the ability to cope. Next, Svartdal distinguishes between so-called problem-focused coping, whereby the individual does something active and problem-solving about the challenge itself, and emotionally focused coping whereby the individual instead does something about the experience or the emotions that the problem creates. Furthermore, *self-efficacy* refers to the belief in one's own abilities and resources that are assumed to be important in dealing with different performance situations. Self-regulation is also highlighted as it addresses an individual's regulation of behaviour, thoughts and emotions related to a goal the individual has set for himself/herself. Svartdal also includes attribution and control, as coping often concerns whether we attribute a good or poor performance to our own abilities or to something involving the situation. Finally, Svartdal refers to the characteristic of *grit* and the associated *fixed mindset*, which is used as an explanation for why a person interprets a bad result fatalistically ("I don't have the abilities and will never succeed") or operates with more dynamic explanations ("I just haven't learnt it yet") – a so-called learning mindset (*growth mindset*) – which increases the chance that the person will try again.

The terms Svartdal introduces – resilience, self-efficacy, self-regulation, grit and learning mindset – represent some of the foremost psychological salutary expressions in recent years. They stem from traditions in psychological research and are less formalistic than the term "life mastery", which is prescribed in the subject renewal. But it is one thing is to establish that a high degree of psychological resilience, the ability to self-regulate or stand-at-will all seem to be associated with doing well in life and success in achieving goals; it is quite another thing to insist that the sum of these qualities can be taught and cultivated as an individual capacity in children and young people in an interdisciplinary course in life mastery at school. The path to the destination is not always a straight one, even though it may be tempting to see it as such.

Coping as a public health measure

"Stress and coping are words that we surround ourselves with in the everyday language and in concepts that have been topical in recent years", Health Director Bjørn Guldvog commented in 2017 in the investigative report *Into Stress and Coping*.[4] The point at which this realisation that Guldvog is referring occurred is difficult to pinpoint exactly, but it is still possible to track a change of pace in this country from the time between the public health report of 2013 under the social democratic title *Good Health – Joint Responsibility* and the 2015 public health report with the more promising moniker *Coping and Opportunities*.[5] "Responsibilities' has now been replaced with "opportunities". In the latter report to the Storting, coping is also assigned a crucial role in the public health of Norwegians: "But good health is not only the absence of disease, it is also about mastering the challenges of life. Mastery and coping give joy, meaning and energy, even when we are struck by illness".[6] Although not explicitly mentioned, it is obvious that this is the famous 1948 definition of health from the World Health Organization (WHO) – "A state of complete physical, mental and social well-being and not just absence of illness or physical impairment"[7] – as implicitly referred to here. The WHO definition has been duly criticised for postulating health as an almost unattainable standard, which in reality is more reminiscent of a secular form of salvation. A permanent state of happiness that will be utopian for most people. Therefore, the report to the Storting more soberly states that it is possible to live a vital and meaningful life even though it is not necessarily always illness-free. This sounds well and good, but at the same time, the public health report entails a shift from its predecessors' insistence on responsibility as a common concern to an understanding of responsibility as something that rests with the individual. This is closely associated with the introduction of coping as a public health measure:

> The basis is that adults must take responsibility for their own life and health. At the same time, we know that health and quality of life are shaped

by conditions that are beyond the control of the individual and it leads to different conditions for freedom and responsibility. An important element of public health policy is strengthening the individual. It involves creating conditions for mastering challenges and taking advantage of the opportunities that life offers. It is about finding the right balance between the responsibility of individuals for their own life and the responsibility of the authorities to create the most equal conditions.[8]

The next public health report with the more vapid title *Good Life in a Safe Society*, published in 2019, established in the introduction that the challenges are essentially the same as they were in 2015. The coping perspective is not overarching as in the previous report, but five years later, it has seemingly been seamlessly absorbed into public health work and therefore no longer needs to be emphasized as much. However, one of the commitments of the health and life skills initiative, which will be one of three priority interdisciplinary subjects in the renewed curriculum that will come into force from autumn 2020, is highlighted: "The subject is intended to help students acquire competence that promotes good psychological and physical health and that accommodates their right to make responsible life choices".[9] Health and life skills are not reserved solely for adults but will now also provide more young people with opportunities to make good choices inside and outside of school. However, "coping and opportunities" do not come at no cost. The "joint responsibility" has not been formally dissolved but has been defined to a greater extent as an individual responsibility for adults as well as young people.

Major and minor victories and defeats

The most recent public health report also states that several schools are already actively working to introduce life mastery skills into teaching in all subjects. In this respect, reference is made to the report *Life Mastery in Schools: Various Major and Minor Victories in Everyday Life* was commissioned by the Government and prepared by the Norwegian Children and Youth Council on its behalf to specify the further work to be done. In the introduction to the report for which investigators spoke to 200 children and young people, 21 child and youth organizations and a number of professionals and ancillary driving forces, it is stated that:

> An inability to cope with the challenges of life can be seen as a leading cause of mental health issues, which is a currently growing problem for children and young people. This is confirmed in the latest investigations from NOVA 'Youth in Oslo 2015' and Ungdata 2015 and 2016.[10]

This alleged causal relationship between increased mental health issues and lack of coping illustrates that in a short period of time, the coping perspective has manifested itself as an obvious framework for understanding the challenges facing children and young people in Norway. And with such a diagnostic social basis, it is not surprising that both the young people themselves and their teachers believe that "Young people need to learn tools to better manage everyday life".[11] However, the load is thereby accompanied by the inexorable responsibility along with the risk that life mastery will entail not only major and minor victories for the students but also major and minor defeats. Although it is believed that existing problems require new solutions, it is often also the case that new solutions bring along new problems.

How is mastery of life accomplished?

If we look to the schools at the time of this writing, a few months before health and life skills are officially implemented, the players, programmes and solution proposals differ even more substantially than the definitions of life mastery, if that is at all possible. The proposed new curriculum has also been criticised by professionals for its lack of clear competence aims that help schools manage health and life skills and prioritise mental health.[12] Ergo, it is not surprising that there is some uncertainty about how life skills should be implemented in schools around Norway. However, despite the lack of clear guidance from the national education authorities, it is possible to give an outline some examples of life mastery skills programmes that are in use. Overall, they are able to reveal how the subject is currently being interpreted and implemented.

In collaboration with Trondheim municipality and two local schools, NTNU has developed the programme *Life Mastery on the Schedule: Education in Mental Health* (*UPS!*). Here, students have had the life mastery subject *UPS!*, which has taught them about mental health for 25 weeks of a school year aimed at enhancing the knowledge, abilities and skills "that will equip them to take care of their mental health".[13] The results "showed no significant change in the variables of well-being at school, friendship, social support, self-esteem, resilience and thoughts of the future before and after UPS!",[14] but students cited increased coping and knowledge about mental health, as they say they know what they can do to reduce stress, change from negative to positive thoughts, what they can do if they are having difficult thoughts and emotions and where they can get help with them. At the same time, the results show an increase in subjective mental health issues among students after *UPS!*, but the explanation given is "that 25 weeks of life mastery education has failed to prevent the increase in mental health issues that we are seeing among adolescents in this age group".[15] Thus, there is a need for more, and the majority of the students interviewed also believe that there should be a separate life skills subject on the timetable.

The Norwegian Centre for Learning Environment and Behavioural Research in Education at the University of Stavanger has developed *Robust*, which is a teaching programme aimed at promoting social and emotional competence, as well as motivation among students in secondary schools. In 20 hours over five days, teachers equipped with a digital course manual will teach students about learning mindsets, regulation of emotions, problem solving, attentive presence and social competence and responsibility. The Learning Mindset programme is about the promotion of the students' belief in their own abilities and prerequisites and highlights "that the brain is like a muscle".[16] An anonymous student who has obviously embraced the quintessence of the programme is quoted in the course folder as follows:

> It's not about anyone being smarter than anyone else but about whether I can become smarter tomorrow than I am today. I now look at school differently. I refuse to let anyone put me into a stall and tell me who I am or how it's going to be with me. It's up to me to do the work needed to increase brain capacity so that I do better at school.[17]

In the 2020/2021 academic year, the plan is to invite 100 teachers in Stavanger, Sandnes and the Jæren area and their year-8 students to participate in the project. *Robust* is also a part of the research project *Resilient*, which has been granted NOK 20 million in funding from the Research Council of Norway.

Modum Bad and Modum Municipality have jointly developed *#psyktnormalt*, (normal psyche) a mental health teaching programme for year-8 students consisting of four class hours distributed over four weeks, as well as one lecture for parents and one for teachers.[18] The purpose of the programme is to teach students about different emotions and how to regulate them, to show new ways by which to deal with difficult emotions and thoughts such as rumination and worrying, normalising psychological difficulties and making it easier for students to seek help if they are struggling. The basis of the programme is the realisation that life mastery is essentially an empty construction: "Life mastery is a term that must be filled with content. #psyktnormalt seeks to fill this void".[19]

In collaboration with Østfold County Council, a school in Akershus and Fagakademiet, the Norwegian Institute of Public Health initiated *The Power of Thought – A Life Mastery Programme* that is currently being tested in ten schools, with around 2,400 students in the first stage of upper secondary school around the Eastern Norway region.[20] In addition to physical health, students will learn how they can improve their mental health – so-called "mind gym" – once a week for a 90-minute session each time over ten weeks. The subjects referred to in the information sheet are *mindfulness*, positive psychology and cognitive method. The programme is referred to as general knowledge in line with maths and Norwegian and does not have an exam, but homework is expected through exercises between each session. The unique aspects of *The Power of Thought* in this context is that it will follow students for up to 15 years afterwards, looking at things such as completed education, choice of profession and work participation. As the initiators admit: "No one, either abroad or in Norway, has tested the measure as a general measure for all school classes".[21]

Forandringsfabrikken (The Change Factory) is an ideal foundation that works to ensure that the schemes for children and young people in Norway are perceived as safe and useful. To acquire knowledge about this, Forandrings-fabrikken collects the perceptions and advice from children and young people via a participative research method called Participatory Learning and Action. It is the same for life mastery. In *The LIFE Hour – Student Proposals for Life Mastery*, Forandringsfabrikken has developed an educational scheme that is already in use in a number of schools around the country.[22] The key message is that *The LIFE Hour* should be an hour in which students can talk about important subjects and learn about and from each other by expressing emotions in words and talking about them. The teaching programme *The LIFE Hour* is reminiscent of self-help groups for which the goal is for everyone to participate by sharing something personal and where what is shared remains in the group and is not to be talked about outside. The teaching folder quotes an anonymous teacher from Bergen reassuring worried parents: "Many adults are afraid that things may come out in the ring that can be used against vulnerable students in retrospect. I've never experienced this".[23] At Ammerud School in Oslo, where the scheme has been used, parents were nevertheless recently warned that some students have felt pressured to share things with the class, so it is clearly not entirely unproblematic, although the teachers here also believe that the class environment has been improved by the life mastery measure.[24]

The Psychology Students' Informative Education Work for Youth (POFU) organisation was started in 2016 in collaboration with Youth Mental Health under model of the Medisinernes seksualopplysning organisation (Medical students' sex education organisation). In the same way that medical students provide young people with sexual education information, psychology students wanted to teach year-9 students about mental health. After initially receiving funding from the Extrastiftelsen (Extra Foundation), the organization was then allocated three million over the state budget for 2018 and 2019. By January 2019, more than a hundred volunteer psychology students in Oslo, Bergen, Trondheim and Tromsø had taught more than 5,000 students nationwide. Students will learn about thoughts and feelings, everyday habits to look after their own mental health and how they can notice that the problems are becoming too big or too many, and then what they can do about it. The teaching alternates between practical exercises and short lectures. In these, it is communicated that we must work actively ourselves to take care of our mental health in order to be well:

> We've started talking about the mental health, which we all have. And just as we have to take care of our physical health, we must maintain the psychological aspect. . . . So to be well, it is necessary to help ourselves.[25]

At the same time, it is emphasised that the problems can sometimes become too great and that one should then seek help from others. The teaching programme appears well thought out and was developed in consultation with professionals but nevertheless contains controversial psychological techniques such as *power posing* and positive self-talk.

The Regional Resource Centre on Violence, Traumatic Stress and Suicide Prevention – RTVS South – has prepared a dedicated teacher guide for life mastery in Norwegian classrooms – *LINK* – which recommends a total of 30 student gatherings divided into the subjects, "Emotions school", "Me and the others" and "For better and worse".[26] In the academic supervision for what might resemble the class meeting hour, where the seating is often a horseshoe, an age-specific progression is outlined, from subjects such as feelings of joy and anger and being a good friend in year 1 to sexual abuse and the meaning of life in year 10. The purpose is to strengthen the self-image of the individual student, contribute to an increased experience of belonging and provide training in constructive coping strategies. The supervisor provides the following rationale for why the school needs life mastery:

> What sets LINK apart from other school programmes is that we want to look behind the behaviour of the individual child. The current challenge landscape shows a generation of youth that is very well functioning. Many people do well at school, they work in their spare time, eat healthily, exercise, get high less than before and the use of violence among young people a [sic] is declining. Meanwhile, 30% struggle with depressive symptoms, 25% say they have deliberately harmed themselves and 10% say they have tried to take their own lives. So we don't need better children and young people. We need happier children and young people.[27]

The source here is the Youth in Agder survey, but the picture drawn in the *LINK*-guide of a generation of youth that is very well functioning but at the same time plagued by symptoms of depression, self-harm and suicidality, conveys the underlying message that this is the same youth and not the youth at either end of the spectrum. It is debatable, but with such a perception it is not surprising that the social medicine prescribed is to help *everyone* deal with life.

In autumn 2019, NRK Skole, which supplies materials for use in teaching, launched fifty video clips in the series *In Short – Life Mastery*, in which two-minute long animation films explain things including brain development, willpower, self-image, self-esteem, joy, fear, shame and guilt. The series is considered to be both a tool for teachers and something that young people can seek out for themselves and also alternates between typical psycho-educative subjects such as "Brain Development" and "What are emotions?", to more directly inviting subjects widely known from self-help literature, such as "What do you want from your life?" and "Reach your goals!". This excitement is also expressed by the fact that mental health becomes something *you* can master. The episode "What is mental health?" starts with the relatively sombre, updated health definition from WHO: "A state of well-being in which the individual realises their opportunities, can handle normal life stress, can work in a fruitful and productive way, and has the opportunity to contribute to society".[28] But the presenter then adds: "Or we can express it more simply: Mental health is about how we manage dealing with what happens in everyday life".[29] The ethos of cognitive therapy also shines through in some of the other self-help videos: "Even if you can't control the thoughts that are coming, you can still influence which thoughts gain a place".[30] It is well established that the way we think can affect our emotional and physical reactions, but cognitive therapy can also be criticised for placing too much emphasis on how we feel being largely something we choose ourselves. In the episode "What is a thought?" the narrator says:

> It is usual to have both light and dark thoughts. The light should be given the most space. They make life easier and make you happy. They create development and progress. If the dark thoughts get the biggest place, they can become very troublesome.[31]

It is not unreasonable to interpret this as that the individual must sort between light and dark thoughts himself/herself and should choose to cultivate the light thoughts, as they make life easiest. Nothing is said here about the fact that *some* children and young people will necessarily produce more dark thoughts than others because their life situation is more difficult. Children have different circumstances in which they grow up. Nor is it said that this is the responsibility of the adults, as pointed out by special education teacher Gunhild Nordvik Reite when commenting on the series:

> I haven't seen that it has been made crystal clear for children that when you are exposed to bad experiences that give you bad thoughts, the most important thing is that adults sort it out, not that you learn to think in a better way.[32]

Life mastery is also not reserved only for schoolchildren. In the last national curriculum for kindergarten and daycare, it is also established that: "Kindergarten and daycare will promote democracy, diversity and mutual respect, equality, sustainable development, life mastery and health".[33] The kindergarten or daycare facility is to ensure that children experience well-being, joy of life, coping and a sense of self-worth and prevent abuse and bullying. Beyond these rules, the national curriculum says little about how life mastery should be implemented. In the book *Life Mastery and Mental Health*, educators May Britt Drugli and Ratib Lekhal aim to give kindergarten and daycare facility employees an introduction to life mastery with the youngest children.[34]

Notably, the section on life skills is the shortest in the book. The short chapter of three pages is mostly about the concept of life mastery as it is expressed in the governance document for schools. Drugli and Lekhal do not make any negative mention of life mastery but do not seem to think that it changes anything about the lack of kindergarten content: "As we see it, this [mental health and life mastery] is not about introducing something new to the work with the children but first and foremost, is about working systematically with good quality kindergartens and daycare facilities".[35] For now, life mastery in kindergarten and daycare facilities seems to exist mostly on paper.

Life mastery seems to permit a wide range of psychological concepts and techniques. There are already several books on the market that seek to fill the subject with content. These include Anne Sælebakke's *Life Mastery in School: A Relational Perspective*, in which, as the title suggests, she presents a relational perspective on life mastery, which can be developed through training in mindful presence, also referred to as *mindfulness*.[36] Sælebakke initially admits that it is "not entirely clear what lies in the term life mastery".[37] But with the backing of the definition of relational competence from Jan Spurkeland – "skills, abilities, knowledge and attitudes that establish, develop, maintain and repair relationships between people"[38] – she emphasises that both teachers and students can train and develop this ability as a basis for life mastery. However, learning relationship skills must always start with strengthening the relationship that you have with yourself. And to achieve that, we need *mindfulness* according to Sælebakke, who is the former head of the association Mindfulness Norway. The logical consequence is that all participants in schools, teachers and pupils, should first learn *mindfulness*, then learn to strengthen the relationship they have with themselves, then learn relationship skills and then learn life mastery. Everything can apparently be reduced to everything within the life mastery spectrum in school.

The obscure essence of life also entails that psychological self-help techniques may have resurrected life both inside and outside the school. In 2019, NRK visited Lier upper secondary school where students have already started a life skills course in physical education classes. Teacher Anette Kyvik, pictured sitting reclining with her hands behind her head and her legs on the table, argues that tools such as *power posing* can produce good results for young people: "They can thereby regulate their emotions with specific actions".[39] The method Kyvik is illustrating only initially became known after the journal *Psychological Science* published a study that showed that merely changing body position when speaking in front of gathering or sitting in a job interview can not only make you feel more confident but even stimulate bodily production of testosterone.[40] But when something sounds too good to be true, it usually is, and later replications have not found evidence to support that *power posing* produces hormonal or behavioural changes but that the technique can give an increased sense of power.[41] This effect is also contested and may be due to the expectation of an effect on the part of the participants.[42] The first author behind the study has since publicly distanced herself from it, but not the second author, psychologist Amy Cuddy, who defended in a new scientific paper in 2018 the effect that different bodily poses might have in making people feel more powerful.[43] Although said the final word has yet to be spoken concerning *the scientific basis for power posing*, its appeal is indisputable. Cuddy's "Fake it till you make it"-inspired TED talk is the second most watched show in the history of the series, with 57 million views. Despite the fascination, the question is asked whether it is not more "fake" than "make" when Cuddy, against a backdrop of Wonder Woman, ends by telling the weak of the world that *power posing* for just two minutes "can significantly change the outcome of their lives".[44] In Lier, however, Kyvik's students seem to be satisfied with the mastery of life they are learning, and when reading between the lines, one gets the sense that the positive and cognitive psychology has already left its mark:

> Fahran Alzayegh believes that it is only the skilled that manage to focus on the positive through everyday ups and downs. Life mastery at school can therefore make even more young people "skilled". 'We need to get better at being like a flower in the wind – we have to turn to what happens in life' says Fahran.[45]

In the neighbouring municipality of Drammen, NRK was also present when Crown Prince Haakon inaugurated *Flyt* – "a life mastery programme for young people in the transition to upper secondary school". The aim is to prevent dropping out of school and the programme was started in Drammen, Hurdal, Sarpsborg and Søndre Land in autumn 2019. In the radio segment, one can hear the Crown Prince saying to the young people who had turned up: "So when you get up in the morning and look at yourself in the mirror, it might be nice to say something good to yourself".[46] The Crown Prince follows up with what he could have said himself: "I'm good at taking my kids to activities".[47] The method that Crown Prince Haakon prescribes here is called positive self-talk and is primarily associated with the "love yourself" theme in self-help literature. In 2009, Joanne Wood and colleagues conducted an experiment that examined the effects of positive self-talk for a group of participants with high self-esteem and a group with low self-esteem.[48] For the former, the impact was marginally positive, while for the latter, the results showed that doing exercises such as standing in front of the mirror and repeating loudly to themselves: "I am a person worth loving" could actually make matters worse in many cases. One possible explanation may be that if someone is tormented by some negative thoughts in the first place, exercises in which you think positive thoughts can reinforce the certainty that the distance between the ideal and reality is substantial. Wood outlines such an inner dialogue:

> If I am going to think about how lovable I am in accordance with the instructions and I still think that I'm not worth loving, then the reasons

why I'm not worth loving must be quite important. I am certainly not worth loving.[49]

That is to say that the message "I am a person worth loving" can provoke its own twisted image: "I am a person who needs to stand in front of the mirror and say to myself that I am a person worth loving".[50] In the case of *power posing*, the different body poses admittedly have little effect but they probably do no significant harm, while positive self-talk can actually amplify negative emotions in young people who already have some of these, while the assumed positive effects are marginal. It must be added here that Crown Prince Haakon's *Flyt* programme also includes a number of other factors, such as group exercises in social and emotional competence, the connection between thoughts and feelings, coping with stress and communication and relationships, which are also being assessed by the Fafo Research Foundation.[51] Seen in isolation, it is also not certain that the cases from Viken are so grave but they provide insight into how the willingness to import whatever psychological techniques that may be readily available, whether repudiated or not, is currently greater than the willingness to critically examine these before they are introduced into the everyday lives of children and young people.

Research shows that . . .

At the same time, many of the parties responsible for mental health and life mastery programmes in schools rely on international research. So what does this say? The EU Data Preview project published the first review of more than 52 overview studies of mental health measures implemented in schools, which showed that these had a small to moderate positive effect on anxiety and depression (0.10–0.50), well-being (0.15–0.37), self-esteem and self-confidence (0.34–0.69) and a moderate to large effect on social and emotional competencies (0.5–1.49). The researchers argue that these effects are not insignificant, as the measures target so many children and young people through school.[52] Another meta-study from 2016 that included 144 randomised controlled trials conducted between 1980 and 2014 – 113 of which were in school settings and a total of 46,072 participants – looked at the effects of universal, selective and indicated prevention strategies for anxiety and depression among children and adolescents aged five to 18 years.[53] The results show a slight decrease (0.13 after twelve months) in the incidence of internalising symptoms of anxiety and depression. The fact that the effect is relatively modest can be explained by the fact that with universal measures, most participants will have low levels in the first place and therefore, there is not much to gain measuring only on the basis of magnitude of effect.[54] Again, although the effect is small, it is not insignificant, given the large range of universal measures and estimated duration twelve months later, while the effect of selective and indicated measures lasted for a shorter duration.[55] In a 2017 meta-study, schools looked at programmes intended to reduce anxiety and depression that included 81 individual studies with a total of 31,794 students.[56] Relatively small magnitude of effect for both anxiety (0.20) and depression (0.23) were measured right after the programmes had finished and twelve months later, when the effect was approximately halved (0.13 and 0.11). Nevertheless, with the same reasoning, the researchers conclude that the possibility of reaching so many children and young people and not just a few, suggests that school-based prevention programmes have the potential to reduce the overall mental health burden in the population.

At the same time, the authors admit that more research is needed, not least because there are a multitude of encumbrances in this field of knowledge. Most of the studies that have been done are based on self-reporting rather than clinical studies. There has been a lack of control groups, the effects have been examined over too short a period of time, the number of students in some studies is low and there is generally a risk of only having positive findings published. In addition, the researchers behind a number of individual studies have developed the school programmes themselves and there is a significant variation in what the different health-promoting measures in school have addressed, from hot lunches to cognitive behavioural therapy.

If I were to add another source of error, it is that side effects are taken lightly. In one of the metastudies, the researchers refer to the critics of psychological programmes in schools, specifically the book *The Dangerous Rise of Therapeutic Education* by Kathryn Ecclestone and Dennis Hayes, but at the same time reject it outright: "There were very few examples of negative effects, which is reassuring given some of the concerns that have been raised about the 'dangers' in this area".[57] But Ecclestone and Hayes fear that the school will no longer primarily orient students towards the world but to a greater extent towards themselves.[58] Of course, how well-founded this worry is can be discussed, but what these individual studies are measuring is whether students experience changes in their mental health. Ergo, it's not surprising that the warning from Ecclestone and Hayes passes under the radar. The attempt to take the critics of the therapeutic school seriously is reminiscent of the so-called streetlight effect, in which one night a police officer finds a drunk man is searching for something under a streetlight. The man says he has lost his keys and they both begin searching under the streetlight. After a while, the policeman asks if he is certain that this is where he lost them, whereupon the intoxicated man replies: "No, it was in the park". The policeman then wonders why the man is searching here and the man replies: "This is where the light is".

But despite the reservations: Does life mastery work? If the answer is "yes" without reservation, many of the doubts raised about whether it should be introduced in schools will easily lose relevance. At the same time, it is not uncommon for research to show arguments that narrow down the issue of mental health and life mastery to a purely empirical matter, when there is a strong normative side and research in human sciences always turns up specific underlying human and world views that will always be open to debate.

Notes

1 In the White Paper for the Storting, Report St. 28, *Fag – Fordypning – Forståelse. En fornyelse av Kunnskapsløftet* [*Subject-Specialisation-Understanding: A Renewal of the Knowledge Promotion Reform*] (Oslo: Ministry of Education and Research, 2016).
2 Norwegian Directorate for Education and Training, *Lærerplanverket* [*Curriculum*] (Oslo: Norwegian Directorate for Education and Training, 2020), www.udir.no/lk20/overordnet-del/prinsipper-for-laring-utvikling-og-danning/tverrfaglige-temaer/folkehelse-og-livsmestring/.
3 Frode Svartdal, "Mestring [Coping]", *Store norske leksikon* (2018), https://snl.no/mestring.
4 Oddrun Samdal et al., *Stress og mestring* [*Stress and Coping*] (Oslo: The Norwegian Directorate of Health, 2017), 1.
5 Report to the Storting, Report St. 19, *Folkehelsemesningen. Mestring og muligheter* [*Public Health Report: Coping and Opportunities*], Ministry of Health and Care Services (Oslo, 2014–2015); Report. St. 34, *Folkehelsemeldingen. God helles – felles ansvar* [*Public Health Report: Good Health-Joint Responsibility*], Ministry of Health and Care Services (Oslo, 2012–2013).
6 Report. St. 19., *Folkehelsemeldingen* [*Public Health Report:. Coping and Opportunities*], 9.
7 WHO, "Constitution", *WHO* (2020), www.who.int/about/who-we-are/constitution., sec. 3.
8 Report to the Storting, Report St. 19, *Folkehelsemeldingen. Mestring og muligheter* [*Public Health Report: Coping and Opportunities*], 51.
9 Report. St. 19, *Folkehelsemeldingen. Gode liv eit trygt samfunn* [*Public Health Report: Good Lives in a Safe Society*], Ministry of Health and Care Services (Oslo, 2018–2019), 30.
10 The Norwegian Children and Youth Council, *Livsmestring i skolen: For flere små og store seiere i hverdagen* [*Life Mastery in Schools: Different Small and Large Victories in Everyday Life*] (2017), www.lnu.no/wp-content/uploads/2017/01/lis-sluttrapport-1.pdf, 10.
11 Maria Kommandantvold and Ida Gjellerud, "Slik skal ungdommen lære å mestre hverdagen [How young people learn to cope with everyday life]", *NRK* (2019, 24.4.), www.nrk.no/osloogviken/slik-skal-ungdommen-laere-a-mestre-hverdagen-1.14520405.
12 Arne Holte et al., "Ny lærerplan i skolen uten psykisk helse? Dette kan du ikke leve med, Sanner [New curriculum in schools without mental health? You can't live like this, Sanner]", *Aftenposten* (2019, 12.5.), www.aftenposten.no/meninger/kronikk/i/GGwvGl/ny-laereplan-i-skolen-uten-psykisk-helse-dette-kan-du-ikke-leve-med-sanner.
13 Anne Torhild Klomsten, *Livsmestring på timeplanen: Utdanning i PSykisk helse* [*Life Mastery on the Schedule: Education in Mental Health*] (Trondheim: NTNU, 2018), 4.
14 Ibid., 6.
15 Ibid.
16 The Learning Environment Centre, *Robust* [*Robust*] (Stavanger: University of Stavanger, 2020).
17 Ibid.
18 Sverre Urnes Johnson et al., "Psykisk helse i skolen: #psyktnormalt [Mental health in schools: #pschnormal]", *Utdanningsnytt* (2019, 25.7.), www.utdanningsnytt.no/psykisk-helse/psykisk-helse-i-skolen-psyktnormalt/206298.
19 Ibid., para. 29.
20 Gry Anette Sælid, "Tankekraft – et livsmestringsprogram. Prosjektbeskrivelse [The power of thought: A life mastery programme: Project description]", *Norwegian Institute of Public Health* (2018, 20.11), www.fhi.no/cristin-prosjekter/aktiv/mentale-teknikker-i-hverdagen-mt/.

21 Ibid., sec. 5.
22 The Change Factory, *Timen LIVET – elevers forslag til livsmestring* [*The LIFE Hour: Student Proposals for Life Mastery*] (Oslo: Forandringsfabrikken, 2019).
23 Ibid., 17.
24 Sonja Holterman and Kari Oliv Vedvik, "-Elever har følt seg presset til å dele ting med klassen [Students have felt pressured to share things with the class", *Utdanningsnytt* (2020, 15.3.), www.utdanningsnytt.no/fagfornyelsen-livsmestring/foreldre-reagerer-elever-har-folt-seg-presset-til-a-dele-ting-med-klassen/234166.
25 Joakim Ebeltoft and Vilde Vollestad, *Undervisningsmanual. Psykologistudentenes opplysningsarbeid for unge, 4. utg.* [*Teaching Manual: Psychology Students' Informative Education Work for Youth, 4. ed.*] (Oslo: Psychology Students' Informative Education Work for Youth, 2019), 34.
26 RVTS South, *Lærerveiledning til LINK* [*Teacher's Guide to LINK*] (Kristiansand: RVTS South, 2017).
27 Ibid., 5.
28 NRK Skole, "Hva er psykisk helse? [What is mental health?]", *Briefly Explained: Life Mastery* (NRK, 2019, 5.10.), 0:06.
29 Ibid., 0:17.
30 "Hva er en tanke? [What is a thought?]", *Briefly Explained: Life Mastery* (NRK, 2019, 7.10.), 1:18.
31 Ibid., 1:29.
32 Gunhild Nordvik Reite, "NRKs 'Livsmestring' har bismak [The NRK 'life mastery' has a bad taste]", *Dagbladet* (2019, 13.11), www.dagbladet.no/kultur/nrks-livsmestring-har-bismak/71804799.
33 Norwegian Directorate of Education, *Rammeplan for barnehagen* [*National Curriculum for Kindergarten Daycare Facilities*] (Oslo: Norwegian Directorate of Education, 2017), 7.
34 May Britt Drugli and Ratib Lekhal, *Livsmestring og psykisk helse* [*Life Mastery and Mental Health*] (Oslo: Cappelen Damm Akademisk, 2018).
35 Ibid., 99.
36 Anne Sælebakke, *Livsmestring i skolen. Et relasjonelt perspektiv* [*Life Mastery in School: A Relational Perspective*] (Oslo: Gyldendal Akademisk, 2018).
37 Ibid., 23.
38 Ibid., 34.
39 Kommandantvoldt and Gjellerud, "Slik skal ungdommen lære å mestre hverdagen [How young people will learn to cope with everyday life]."
40 Dana R. Carney, Amy J.C. Cuddy, and Andy J. Yap, "Power posing: Brief nonverbal displays affect neuroendocrine levels and risk tolerance", *Psychological Science* 21, no. 10 (2010).
41 Eva Ranehill et al., "Assessing the robustness of power posing: No effect on hormones and risk tolerance in a large sample of men and women", ibid. 26, no. 5 (2015).
42 Joar Øveraas Halvorsen and Jan-Ole Hesselberg, "Gir pseudovitenskap på timeplanen bedre livsmestring? [Does pseudoscience on the schedule improve life mastery?]", *Aftenposten* (2019, 28.4.), www.aftenposten.no/meninger/debatt/i/VbgvJ4/gir-pseudovitenskap-paa-timeplanen-bedre-livsmestring-halvorsen-og-hesselberg?
43 Amy J.C. Cuddy, S. Jack Schultz, and Nathan E. Fosse, "P-Curving a more comprehensive body of research on postural feedback reveals clear evidential value for power-posing effects", *Psychological Science* 29, no. 4 (2018).
44 Amy Cuddy, "Your body language may shape who you are", *TED* (2012), 20:30.
45 Kommandantvoldt and Gjellerud, "Slik skal ungdommen lære å mestre hverdagen [How young people will learn to cope with everyday life]", sec. 13–14.
46 NRK P2, "Nyhetsmorgen", *News Morning* (2019, 8.10.).
47 Ibid.

48 Joanne V. Wood, W.Q. Perunovic and John W. Lee, "Positive self-statements", *Psychological Science* 20, no. 7 (2009).
49 Ibid.
50 Ibid.
51 Kristin Halvorsen and Irene L. Lystrup, "Kronprinsparets Fond svarer på kritikken: De unge lærer mange ulike strategier for å mestre livet bedre [The crown prince and crown princess' foundation responds to the criticism: The young people learn many different strategies for a better mastery of life]", *Aftenposten* (2019, 15.10.), www.aftenposten.no/meninger/debatt/i/GG88Mx/kronprinsparets-fond-svarer-paa-kritikken-de-unge-laerer-mange-ulike-strategier-for-aa-mestre-livet-bedre-kristin-halvorsen-og-irene-l-lystrup.
52 Katherine Weare and Melanie Nind, "Mental health promotion and problem prevention in schools: What does the evidence say?", *Health Promotion International* 26, no. suppl_1 (2011).
53 Emily Stockings et al., "Preventing depression and anxiety in young people: A review of the joint efficacy of universal, selective and indicated prevention", *Psychological Medicine* 46, no. 1 (2016).
54 Arne Holte, "Forebygging av depressive plager hos barn og unge – på tvers av arenaer [Prevention of depressive problems in children and adolescents: Across arenas]", *Psykologisk.no* (2019, 23.4.), https://psykologisk.no/2019/04/forebygging-av-depressive-plager-hos-barn-og-unge-pa-tvers-av-arenaer/.
55 Stockings et al., "Preventing depression and anxiety in young people: A review of the joint efficacy of universal, selective and indicated prevention."
56 Aliza Werner-Seidler et al., "School-based depression and anxiety prevention programs for young people: A systematic review and meta-analysis", *Clinical Psychology Review* 51 (2017).
57 Weare and Nind, "Mental health promotion and problem prevention in schools: What does the evidence say?", i63.
58 Kathryn Ecclestone and Dennis Hayes, *The Dangerous Rise of Therapeutic Education* (London: Routledge, 2008).

2 Life mastery in context

One of the great pioneers in the field of psychology was German philosopher Wilhelm Dilthey (1833–1911). He was interested in how psychology extended between the natural sciences and the intellectual sciences, each of which had its distinctive research methods.[1] The natural scientific method involved reducing the subject of the investigation down to its smallest constituents, while on the other hand, the intellectual scientific method consisted of the converse: Contextualising and placing a phenomenon into wider contexts. The former procedure seeks causal explanations while the latter approach seeks the greatest possible understanding. Dilthey believed that the intellectual scientific method was most suited to studying the human consciousness, which was the subject of psychology. And as the phenomenon of life mastery cannot be clearly defined, there is reason to believe that Dilthey would have prescribed the intellectual scientific method in order to investigate it further. If we put life mastery into a historical, cultural, political and ideological context, it can help us understand why it has come into the school timetables for children and young people.

Life mastery as prevention

Life mastery can be seen in recent years as part of an increased focus on health promotion and preventive work, not least in psychology.[2] The purpose of saving the individual from afflictions and society from unnecessary treatment costs is basically not difficult to support. But as always, when one begins digging into the good intentions, one finds, if not a direct path to hell, then at least detours that without a doubt lead the wrong way.

In Norway, one of the foremost advocates for adoption of the school as a preventive arena in mental health has been Arne Holte, professor emeritus of health psychology at the University of Oslo and former deputy director, faculty director and divisional director for mental health at the Norwegian Institute of Public Health. Holte cites the British epidemiologist Geoffrey Rose (1926–1993) as a source of inspiration for his support of prevention as a public health measure.[3] Rose's view is based on the perspective that if

DOI: 10.4324/9781003372547-2

the risk of the disease is widespread, measures that reduce risk for the entire population will be more effective than more pointed measures targeted at individuals, even if they have a significantly elevated risk of developing disease.[4] The reason is that the proportion of individuals at increased risk constitutes a numerical minority, while the number of individuals at low or medium risk can be very high. Thus overall, universal prevention measures aimed at everyone will contribute to a greater reduction of the overall burden of the disease. Rose's approach has had a major impact on public health work in recent times but there is also criticism of his population strategy, which is relevant to the issue of health and life skills in the schools.

One of the objections is based on the fact that despite there having been a significant improvement in public health in the West in the last half century, a growing number of studies show that inequality in public health is also increasing.[5] This is problematic, given that prevention measures aimed at the entire population are intended to improve *everyone's* health. Researchers such as Katherine Frohlich and Louise Potvin highlight that people from vulnerable groups in society are less able to respond positively to population-oriented interventions.[6] It is the resourceful individuals who will gain the most benefit from these measures. Another important factor appears to be whether the preventive measures require a little or a lot from the recipients.[7] The health benefits of introducing a smoking law banning smoking in public places will turn out to be more or less the same, while information campaigns on the dangers of smoking will benefit those in the population who are more resourceful and more readily receptive to government advice.

Transferring this thought to life skills in schools invites the notion that the students who are resourceful and already self-regulating will benefit the most from it, not least because the teaching situation requires considerable personal effort in itself. In the worst case it can amplify the differences between students. Resources that could have been earmarked for weak groups are now being made available to everyone and there is much to suggest that those who already have a lot will benefit from it the most. Frohlich and Potvin argue that to a greater extent, work should be undertaken that is purposefully targeted at vulnerable groups in society to counter the counteract the inherent amplification of inequality that public health work has unintentionally caused.[8] They also point out how many of the root causes of health inequalities lie outside the health sector, so that initiatives for vulnerable groups must necessarily also include social, political and economic conditions.

Physician Bruce Charlton has also raised significant objections to both Rose's and health authorities' confidence in population-oriented prevention strategies.[9] Charlton initially disputes the claims that recent improvements in public health are due to prevention programmes. It is difficult to know whether improved public health is due to distinct strategies, and not to other factors such as improved living conditions. Moreover, to be sure, randomised trials would be required to compare one population that receives preventive measures to a control population that does not. It would be very difficult to implement from both a purely practical and ethical research perspective. Charlton's next objection is normative but is supported by the uncertainty that is associated with the effect of prevention measures. Charlton points to Rose's drawing parallels to treatment situations in which diagnosis and treatment are based only on reasonable assumptions that they will do more benefit than harm. However, Charlton points out a difference between treatment and prevention situations. Treatment has an optional basis, in which a sick person asks for help, whereas with prevention, it is a different situation. As a rule, we are usually dealing with healthy people who have *not* asked for help and who have *not* entered into a voluntary relationship with a preventive agency. If prevention is to satisfy fundamental ethical demands, the requirements for expected outcomes must be tightened: "Without such a knowledge requirement, there will be no limit to the kind of lifestyle changes the state can place on the population in the hope of improving health".[10] Charlton also argues that prevention must be considered as more of a political issue than purely a health issue. Many of the requirements that apply to policy measures should therefore also apply to preventive measures. For example, good intentions are far from enough for the imposition of compulsory interventions on a non-consenting population. In this respect, the expected effect, even if it is a necessary condition, will also be insufficient in itself, as it is not possible to automatically assume that improved public health is the overall goal of the policy. Health must instead be balanced against other principles such as justice, freedom and happiness. Charlton still cautions against designating entire populations too sick, as Rose does in his influential article "Sick individuals and sick populations",[11] as it implies that no one can be considered healthy and thus no one is exempt from the orders for the preventive medicine. The idea of a sick population risks medicating people's lives and rendering the concept of health meaningless outside the context of political rhetoric.

So what do Charlton's objections mean for health and life skills? A lot. The question of how good the scientific evidence is that life mastery should be introduced in the schools is of course important but is far from sufficient for determining whether it should be implemented. So while we presuppose that life mastery has lasting and beneficial effects on the psyche of children and young people, which is currently purely hypothetical, Charlton shows how this cannot be reduced to a matter of mental health alone. It also involves other questions, such as: What should the school be? And where it is also possible to envision other interdisciplinary subjects that could be introduced with supposed good consequences but the effect of which does not necessarily concern the mental health of children and young people. There is a lack of good alternatives here: Arts and crafts and movement, play and outdoor activities have all been suggested.[12]

In addition, there is a question of the potential side effects of preventive measures. Charlton's concerns about increased medicalisation also has implications for health and life skills in schools, where it is not possible to get past the related phenomenon of psychology. An underlying question is whether pupils who are exposed to health and life skills will be more or less likely to overload the offices of GPs and psychologists during school hours or afterwards. The official view is that they will be *less* inclined due to trust in the systematic training in school in health and life skills that enables young people to develop their psychological immune system and different coping techniques, which makes them more resilient and thus less reliant on help. On the other hand, sceptics fear that young people will be *more* inclined to do so, due to the students having gained an increased awareness of psychological disorders through teaching, which makes it easier than before to interpret internal and external signals based on a psychiatric diagnostic language.[13] Thus, there the initiatives in school for the mental health of children risk becoming a self-fulfilling prophecy. The results from Trondheim, where students reported several health problems after life skills can be interpreted in such a pattern. *UPS!* suddenly has another possible meaning. At the same time, it is also possible to object: "But no one chooses to get sick!".[14] No, but it is easy to understand how diagnostic categories like anxiety and depression are not only descriptions of symptoms but can also constitute interpretive frameworks that young people can use to understand themselves and their surroundings. People have always used the language that is accessible in contemporary culture to understand their inner life. And when culture becomes a culture of diagnosis[15] or a therapeutic culture, it will,[16] inexorably, also characterise self-understanding of good and evil or more precisely, of sick and healthy. In the next instance, it can increase the likelihood that young people will seek out a psychologist or GP. It is not unreasonable to imagine cases of both minor and major outcomes. But then it must be assumed that the introduction of preventive measures such as health and life skills does not come without potentially undesirable side effects. Moreover, this must at least be assessed against supposed positive effects before being introduced. However, the debate over mental health and life skills in schools in Norway has little to do with such cost-benefit analysis. And it is tempting to speculate that the reason is that one wouldn't like the outcome.

The will to master life

There is much to suggest that life skills in schools became a reality after combined pressure over time from a number of actors from psychological, political and educational ranks, both nationally and internationally. A common denominator appears to be a united concern for children and young people. Throughout the 2010s, there were rising concerns amongst the Norwegian public about the living conditions and mental health of children and young people, in line with mounting reports of mental health issues. The influential Ungdata surveys conducted by NOVA show that throughout the 2010s, Norwegian students in lower secondary and upper secondary schools were reporting more mental health issues.[17] Reporting by boys was admittedly declining in the first half of the decade, but even there, the measurements from the last couple of years show that there were more than before reporting that "everything is a struggle" and "that they have worried about things too much", while for girls, the increase has gone from a few decimal places each year to a more dramatic increase of several percentage points per year after 2015. Whether the increase testifies to deteriorating living conditions for young people of both sexes or to a greater openness to mental health issues amongst young people, many parents, teachers, health nurses, psychologists, doctors, journalists and politicians are naturally concerned about the next generation. It is therefore tempting to consider health and life skills in schools as a response to these concerns. As a result of the surveys, there was enough momentum gradually building amongst a sufficient number of actors to strongly demand that "something must be done now!".

Psychological will

The whole notion of life mastery can also be seen in the context of leading trends in psychology in the latter half of the 20th century. "Psychology is too good to be reserved for the sick", was the confident statement made by family therapist couple Irving and Miriam Polster in 1973 about the nascent vision that would become central to the positive promises of psychology in the 2000s regarding happiness. Normality was now also standing in the way. And the idea that psychology should not only offer professional help reserved for those who seek help but rather that it is something that everyone can make use of became all the more prominent. In the late 1960s, the motto, *Giving Psychology Away* was first promoted as a democratic, inclusive ideal by George A. Miller, then president of the American Psychology Association.[18] He wanted as many people as possible to participate in what he called the psychological revolution. Psychology should no longer be something that took place exclusively behind closed-therapy doors or research laboratories, reserved for the exclusive few who could pay for it, but instead should now be distributed abundantly to everyone. Miller dreamed that happiness would come down to earth and benefit the individual in keeping with the Enlightenment mindset. Moreover, the psychological revolution could be implemented with everyone acting as empowered citizens and self-governing subjects who took responsibility and experienced the ability to cope in education, career, health and life. On the basis of a scientific mapping of human thoughts and feelings and through each individual acting as their own psychologist, the goal of freedom and happiness, self-realisation and self-optimisation and the absence of suffering would be within reach.

The belief in the redeeming potential of psychology for everyone has also made its mark in Norway, and in a short period of time, the status of psychology has become one of the most visible professions in Norwegian public media. In the comment "No one escapes psychology but it is allowed to try", sociologist Gunnar Aakvaag writes: "There is probably no other scientific discipline or profession today that has had as strong a breakthrough in the Norwegian public as psychology. At the risk of exaggerating, we can speak of a new regime of knowledge".[19] In particular, during the twelve-year presidency of Tor Levin Hofgaard from 2007 to 2019, the Norwegian Psychology Association took on the task of an offensive drive to get psychology out into the population to the greatest extent possible. Hofgaard spoke about these ambitions in an interview:

> Psychology is part of the solution to the challenges of the future in many more fields than health. We are saying – see the potential of psychology; use it – for the good of the whole society. In both the national and global context.[20]

And unlike Miller, who idealistically warned against professional imperialism, despite a strong belief in the excellence of psychology: "We don't dare to assume that what is good for psychologists is always good for humanity",[21] and dared his Norwegian colleagues to assume it. The principles programme of the Norwegian Psychology Association states that the activity is "a political interest, a political subject and a sociopolitical organisation" and that these three elements support each other.[22] This can hardly be understood in any way other than that the greater the space psychology gets in society, the better for the population *and* for the psychologists. There is simply no room for questioning the (self)-appointed role of psychology in society in professional thinking. With such a political subject as the basis, it becomes easy to find arguments, *in favour,* for example, of mental health and life mastery in schools, and it appears similarly difficult, if not inconceivable, to find counterarguments.

Therefore, it is not surprising that the stakeholder organizations also went into the breach for life mastery without a single visible reservation. In 2015, the Norwegian Psychology Association spearheaded the campaign, *The Book That is Missing*, which was also supported by actors such as the Norwegian Association of Graduate Teachers, the Norwegian Council for Mental Health, the Norwegian Psychiatric Association, Mental Helse Ungdom and the School Student Union of Norway.[23] A black hole is opening up in front of backpacks, globes and PCs on the cover page of the announcement: "There is a HOLE in the school curricula." Inside the folder, it goes on to say:

> For generations, the school has taught students about physical health. Physical activity and nutrition have been central themes in the teaching. The purpose of all teaching is to give children the tools to be able to manage in life. But the ABCs of thoughts, emotions and actions are not found in the schoolbag.

IT IS NOT JUST A PITY – IT IS INCOMPREHENSIBLE.

Children and young people need knowledge in order to understand themselves and make good choices in life. This is a central part of the general education project of the school. Knowledge that provides maps and a compass for the mental terrain are tools of benefit and cheerfulness for the rest of their lives – as independent individuals, parents, cohabitation partners, work colleagues and citizens.

Good mental health is the most important building block for a good life. It is the basis for good self-esteem, capacity to care and the experience of life mastery. And it contributes to the fight against bullying and to the development of a good psychosocial school environment.

That is why we believe the subject must be given a place in education – in all the schools around the country. We therefore challenge the Minister of Education Torbjørn Røe Isaksen:

WE WANT MENTAL HEALTH TO BE IN THE CURRICULUM!
ONLY THEN WILL WE GET A SCHOOL FOR EVERY PERSON.
ONLY THEN WILL THE SCHOOLBAG BE COMPLETE.[24]

If one interprets the announcement benignly, the initiative can be understood as part of an ongoing development in which the time is now overripe for the psyche to be given the same legitimate status as the body. And where our inner life has been neglected for many years and mental illnesses were things to be kept silent and not be talked about ("Just something to do with nerves"). While for generations the body has been fostered physically and given the right nutrition in subjects such as physical education and home economics, it is time to give the psyche the same status and get mental health and life skills into the curriculum. Based on the prevailing political subject notion that the potential of psychology is only positive, there are therefore no conceivable reasons for not giving children and young people tools in terms of thoughts, feelings and actions so that they can understand themselves better and make good choices later in life.

Political will – a seed is sown

However, the psychological will alone was not enough to get mental health and life skills onto the school timetable; the initiative was also dependent on political will. A couple of days before the national meeting of the Young Christian Democrats Party in Trondheim in May 2015, the leader of their youth party at the time, Emil André Erstad, wrote the comment, "The Young Christian Democrats Party will take a stand against the achievement society".[25] The Young Christian Democrats party thereby launched its countermeasures against "The so-called achievement society [that] is making young people sick".[26] Erstad was referring to the NOVA Ungdata surveys revealing that many young people between the ages of 13 and 17 are plagued by worries and feel that everything is very hard work. Erstad portrays how the young people of Norway today "are gagged by stress and pressure in every-day life"[27] and argues that it doesn't matter if we are the best in the world in sports or mathematics if the pressure to be good means that young people lose themselves and the belief that they are worth just as much no matter how they perform. The Young Christian Democrats therefore proposes "three measures that we want to highlight in order to reduce pressure and stress amongst young people: focus on mental health in school, life mastery on the school timetable and an anti-bullying ombudsman".[28]

Why exactly did this rising unrest erupt amongst the Young Christian Democrats? – presumably, because the demands of the achievement society conflict with Christian values, where everyone is created in the image of God and is considered equally valuable. However, in the production-driven achievement society, *some* people are worth more than others. It is debatable, of course, whether Erstad and his like-minded followers are correct in their diagnosis of the contemporary achievement society as representative of Norway. If one concurs, however, there is little doubt that human dignity is often distributed on the basis of achievement and is somewhat changeable, that is to say dependent on the demand, rather than human dignity being immutable and common to all people from cradle to grave, regardless of the level of work and level of function.[29] With the advent of social media in the lives of young people over the past decade, technological platforms have been created with quantifiable popularity indicators that show the number of followers and likes, further adding to the concerns. A few days later, the parent party of the Young Christian Democrats promised to listen to the youth party and put forward proposals in the Storting on life mastery in schools in accordance with the model from The Cultural Schoolbag. The Young Christian Democrats initiative shows that the political initiative for life skills in schools arose in response to the concerns raised by the achievement society, stress and pressure in the everyday lives of people and in the Ungdata surveys.

Pastoral care

The anxiety about what the achievement society does to us – both young and old – is something the Young Christian Democrats could reasonably expect would resonate with the parent party. If we look to the choice of path for the Christian Democratic Party from last year on whether to collaborate with the government on the right or left, we again find a pronounced concern for the pursuit of achievement in both the left and right wings of the party. In an interview with the Hareide couple about the demanding autumn of 2018, primary school teacher Lisa Maria Hareide speaks of their conversations along the way:

> We talk about school policy a lot. About the achievement society. About how wrong we think the six-year reform has turned out to be. Of course, that's not how it was supposed to be – it was supposed to be fun.[30]

And when Kjell Ingolf Ropstad, the new Christian Democratic Party leader, spoke at his first national meeting the day after he was elected leader, he expressed that these challenges do not concern only the young: "I think we represent a lot of parents who feel like we are not achieving enough. It's not just young people who can feel what they call generation achievement, there's a lot of 'family achievement' as well".[31] Just like the sorting society, which deals with ethical issues at the entrance and exit of life, the achievement society apparently fills a unifying function for the Christian Democratic Party as an external enemy, where the same concerns arise but *in* life: In everyday life, in the school system and in working life. And in both cases, the party seems to think that what people need first and foremost is more support and academic supervision.

Therefore, it was probably not coincidental that first the Young Christian Democrats Party and then the parent party were the initiator of life mastery in schools. Perhaps it would have been proposed sooner or later by another party, but the leading Christian Democratic Party in Norway, founded in 1933, was probably at the forefront as a reaction to the increasing secularisation of society because of its particular sensitivity to directionless youth. A widespread and constant perception among the primary electorate of the Christian Democratic Party is that modern man is directionless and confused in an ever increasingly secularised world, much like "sheep without a shepherd" as spoken of when Jesus meets the crowd in the Gospel of Mark.[32] For example, one of the morning prayers of the Lutheran Confessional Church states: "The people of our time are also like sheep without a shepherd. They have no one to lead them. They wander around a spiritual desert with no purpose and meaning in life".[33] And it is the plight of young people in particular that seems to invoke this parable. In the comment "Generation achievement needs to be brought to life", Daniel Sæbjørnsen from *Faith & Media* speaks of the "sheep without a shepherd" – the grounds for relevance to youth:

> Some time back, I read the Apostle Matthew's depiction of Jesus before a large crowd, in which he writes: "But when He (Jesus) saw the multitudes, he was moved with compassion on them because they fainted and were scattered abroad, as sheep having no shepherd" (9: 36).
>
> Immediately after having read the verses, I thought to myself: "This also describes the people of today and perhaps especially the youth generation". Yes, because is it not fair to say that this generation of young people also seems to be exhausted by all the demands placed on them?[34]

The Christian understanding of the life challenges of generation achievement implies a conviction that their problems are due to the fact that their human dignity can no longer be taken for granted but is now contingent on achievement. A logical consequence of the death of God is that the guarantee of human dignity for everyone also disappears. People are instead made responsible for their own human dignity. In Vårt Land, in a commentary on the TV2 series *Perfectly Sick* about being young today, Margunn Serigstad Dahle, senior lecturer at NLA, writes that the series is actually an expression of a larger current trend:

> Because when individualism forms the centre, we are left to ourselves to the deepest extent – even when the question of self worth comes up. When the relationship with God is gone, there is an individual responsibility for identity and value. The text in small print under many contemporary messages about creating the best version of ourselves is difficult to spot but easy to experience: You are not given a value, you have to create it by performing to perfection.[35]

Therefore, it is perhaps not so surprising that the largest Christian party in Norway – the Christian Democratic Party – was the first to express concern for the youth of today. Many in and around the Christian Democratic Party are inclined to understand the notes of concern about young people as the latest confirmation of the pitfalls of secularisation and in line with the biblical warning of sheep without a shepherd. The generation that is growing up is left to itself and its achievement without anyone watching over them. The party has also been no stranger to proposing shepherd schemes in the past, as when in the wake of the Selective Abortion Act, it went to great lengths to introduce an abortion board and a mandatory waiting period. With the increasing dilution of Christian education and the purpose of the Christian mission probably becoming a lost cause in the long run, and given the slow but steady decline in the belief in God in the population, one might wonder whether life mastery in school will become something of a secular consolation to the party and a winning political banner cause with broad support. But it is also possible to find the same way of thinking as that of the Christian Democratic Party amongst secular supporters of life mastery. Philosopher Ole Martin Moen admits that although he professes atheism, "the need for life mastery in schools increases in line with the secularisation of society".[36] Moen highlights how religion also has so much more space than superstition and "instead of omitting life wisdom and life mastery when society is secularised, we should use knowledge of psychology to fill the void".[37]

Processing by the Storting

Barely one year later on 12 April 2016, the acting chair of the Standing Committee on Education, Research and Church Affairs, Iselin Nybø, presented a recommendation to the Storting in accordance with the suggestion of Christian Democratic Party Storting representatives, Olaug Bollestad, Hans Fredrik

Grøvan, Line Henriette Hjemdal and Anders Tyvand to introduce the project "Life mastery in school" at the lower secondary school level:

Children and young people growing up today are being brought up in a country characterised primarily by stability and prosperity. Nevertheless, many people find that life is difficult to master. They are subject to pressure at school, on the sports team, in their group of friends and at home. Worry, unease and feelings of inadequacy are part of the everyday lives of many of our children and young people, although it is also important to remember that children and young people are mostly thriving and well, not least at school. But there is a need to make room for conversations about different challenges that young people experience in everyday life and to raise awareness amongst students of how such challenges can be mastered. They face challenges in terms of body image pressure, sports performance, school achievement – there are a number of things that children and young people need to talk about today.

The most important task of the school is to give the students knowledge to cope with moving forward in life and in this respect, we are not only talking about academic knowledge such as maths, Norwegian, English, etc., but we are now also talking about becoming cultured and gaining knowledge to cope with life. In schools today we have physical education. We make sure that the students are able to unwind physically and that they learn about how the body works and how we take care of our body and health. However, we are not as good at teaching how we train and take care of our psyche. In this Document 8 proposal, the Christian Democratic Party has promised a project in accordance with the model of the Cultural Schoolbag, with a kind of national competence resource where students will learn about managing life and taking care of themselves.[38]

In the subsequent posts by Christian Tynning Bjørnø (Labour Party), Kent Gudmundsen (Conservative Party), Bente Thorsen (Progress Party), Anders Tyvand (Christian Democratic Party), Anne Tingelstad Wøien (Centre Party) and Cabinet Minister Torbjørn Røe Isaksen (Conservative Party), the motives of the politicians for wanting life mastery in schools becomes clear.

First up, Bjørnø (Labour Party), openly refers to the Ungdata survey from his home county when he explains to the assembly: "In my home county of Telemark, a survey was recently conducted showing that over the last week, almost one-half of all girls have worried a lot and felt that everything is a struggle".[39] Bjørnø also admits to having been influenced by the focus of the media on the difficulties faced by children and young people: "NRK has recently focused on youth and mental health. The strongest impression on me has been the series, *Me Versus Myself*".[40] While Representative Thorsen

(Progress Party) emphasises the expectations of young people of themselves that are too high, aside from body pressure:

> There are many young people today who struggle with low self-esteem, may have too high expectations of themselves and believe that they can and must be number one in large number of areas. In addition, many are subject to body pressure.[41]

Tyvand (Christian Democratic Party) also raises the issue of pressure but in another area:

> (A) pressure to have the newest, most expensive and finest things. This buying pressure is again illustrated by the fact that late payment notices, debt collection cases and debt in the form of consumer loans are a growing trend amongst young people.[42]

Added to this are the glossy images of social media, unrealistic body ideals and bullying. Tyvand also draws in a well-known description of the youth generation:

> The youth generation of today has been called the "achievement generation". Surveys show that many young people feel pressure to succeed academically, socially, physically and financially. Many are left with a feeling of inadequacy, some are dissatisfied with life and some struggle to cope with everyday life.[43]

In 2016, Storting politicians across party lines appear to feel that something needs to be done. Like everyone else, they also sense that children and young people are struggling and "are feeling that they do not measure up" and that this has almost gotten out of hand, at least if one can believe the many disturbing reports from the Ungdata surveys from around Norway, NRK and other media, which serve us the "new openness" about mental illness and give us insight into the struggles faced by young people.

However, in this respect it may be just as interesting to note what is *not* said. If one looks at the debate and the exchange of words in the Storting as a whole, it is clear that the mental health problems faced by young people are discussed without consideration of where the stress and pressure is coming from, who is affected and who is responsible. Instead, the generic descriptions of stress and pressure and of not being good enough are upheld. In the exchange of words between the Minister of Education for the Conservative Party and the Storting representatives from such different parties as the Labour Party, the Centre Party, the Christian Democratic Party, the Liberal Party and the Progress Party, there is almost a touching consensus on the challenges facing children and young people. It is virtually impossible to spot any political dividing lines between the parties or hints of divergent views about the mental difficulties that accompany contemporary demands, based on the various ideological party programmes and values and human views. Nor does the values party par excellence, the Christian Democratic Party, which took the initiative to introduce life mastery into schools, seem to have any further need to emphasise the vigilant, watchful eye of the party for the challenges facing children and young people today as a consequence of increased secularisation. Instead, the Centre Party representative, Anne Tingelstad Wøien, sums up the essence of the debate well when as the final woman speaker, she takes the speaker's rostrum:

> Everyone is upset that so many children and adults are struggling with their lives, feeling bad about themselves and not feeling that they measure up. The question is how we can help improve the students' self-esteem and help them to cope with their lives in other and better ways than they do today. NRK has provided examples to give us a little insight into what many of the young people of today are struggling with. This is a big and difficult issue, which I'm not going to go into further detail with now.[44]

Implied: There is a consensus on being upset that so many young people are struggling with their lives and feeling bad about themselves and feeling that they do not measure up. Everyone wants them to be able to cope with life better but the background for this is so massive and difficult that it should not be explored here. The big and difficult issues are therefore left untouched and instead, life mastery is introduced as a politically neutral instrument that everyone can get behind, regardless of party political affiliation. In front of the Eidsvold painting from 1814, the entire debate about the need for life mastery amongst young people is paradoxically characterised on this April day two hundred years later as being almost apolitical and disconnected from the unique ideological standpoints and different values of the political parties.

Early intervention

When it comes to life mastery, the political will also seems to be rooted in the public health vision of early efforts that were central to the political work in Norway in the 2000s. The principle of early intervention involves "a good educational offer from early childhood, that kindergartens, daycare facilities and schools work to prevent challenges and that measures are implemented immediately when challenges are identified".[45] In other words, educational institutions are given a central place, not least as an arena for the promotion of good mental health. Health and life skills are therefore explicitly mentioned as part of this work. For example, in 2019, the then Minister of Education and Research, Jan Tore Sanner, stated the following:

> We will have a kindergarten, daycare facility and school that provides equal opportunities and uplifts all children regardless of their background. New curricula and early interventions will give students better conditions, and health and life skills are a key part of this.[46]

Remarkably enough, early intervention shares many of the same qualities and shortcomings associated with life mastery. Pedagogue Stine Vik has pointed out that early intervention is

> a principle that most people agree with but that very few of us know what it involves. . . . Nevertheless, early intervention is often referred to as a universal means of fixing everything that is wrong in Norwegian schools, kindergartens and daycare facilities.[47]

In a thematic paper for the Education Association, Senior Adviser Jon Kaurel also points out how despite, or rather because of, the unclear essence of the principle, it has had a broad impact among Norwegian politicians: "Despite the fact that the concept is unclear, early intervention is emphasised in the design of Norwegian education across party political boundaries".[48] Kaurel also points out how the principle is not rooted in a Norwegian pedagogical tradition but is regarded as an import, inspired by the *Early Intervention* and *Head Start* programmes aimed at low-income families who came from the USA in the 1960s. Therefore, early intervention in a Norwegian context must be understood as both politically and professionally initiated.

Pedagogical will

But what about pedagogy, which deals precisely with theoretical and practical questions about teaching, upbringing, learning and development? An obvious educational direction of importance to life mastery is the influential international movement *21st Century Skills*. The movement is even duly introduced in the Official Norwegian Report (NOU) *Student Learning in the School of the Future*, a preliminary report to the later *Ludvigsen Report*, in which life mastery is prescribed.[49] The origins of 21st Century Skills are in the USA at the beginning of the 1980, and in particular the report *A Nation at Risk: The Imperative for Educational Reform*. Here you find a pronounced fear that the US will be outsailed due to increased global competition and that the solution is to be found in a reorientation of the entire education system: "Learning is the necessary investment required to succeed in the age of information that we are entering".[50] In the approaching new era and millennium, the school needs to foster students to learn to a greater extent rather than learning an established content and canned knowledge, as all the facts are now only a keystroke away. Since then, belief in lifelong learning inside and outside school spread to countries such as Canada, New Zealand and the USA and to global economic associations such as APEC, the OECD and the World Economic Forum and technology giants such as Microsoft, Intel and Cisco, which began to voice concerns about being able to recruit new heads from the school desks. Thus, a common basis for the 21st Century Skills seems to be the recognition that economic and technological changes are happening at a faster pace than before, which must have consequences for education. Due to the accelerating development in the 21st century, schools around the world must focus less on the actual content of what is to be taught as it is becoming obsolete faster than before and instead focus all the more on skills. For example, according to the World Economic Forum, 65 per cent of children who are currently attending primary school will end up in professions that do not yet exist. While 47 per cent of existing workplaces will disappear over the next 25 years. Moreover, seven out of ten workers are employed in jobs in which the future of their profession or industry is uncertain. Therefore, we must prepare the education system for jobs and technologies that have not yet been created and encourage students to solve problems that we do not yet know about.[51] The 21st Century Skills are often divided into the following three core areas: Learning skills, which involve critical thinking, creativity, collaboration and communication; textual skills relating to information, media and technology; and life skills, which can involve flexibility, leadership, initiative, productivity and social skills. Internationally, it may seem that the centre of gravity for life skills is primarily associated with the entrepreneurial role in line with roots this educational movement has in economic and technological development, while in the Norwegian learning landscape, health and life skills take up space in this learning pillar.

The Ludvigsen Committee

One of the clearest expressions of this movement in Norway is found in the so-called Ludvigsen Committee. In 2013, the Stoltenberg II Government decided to appoint a committee to look at whether the content of the schools actually covers the skills and competencies that students will need in the society and working life of the future. The public report was led by Professor of Pedagogy Sten Ludvigsen and was presented to the Minister of Education at the time, Torbjørn Røe Isaksen (Conservative Party) just before the summer of 2015 in the form of the report *NOU 2015:8 School of the Future: Renewal of Subjects and Skills*. In the NOU, Isaksen and others were able to read about the ways social development places new demands on students. The Committee has looked to recent research on learning in which an interest is taken in what contributes to learning taking place, in which the feelings, motivation, social skills and relationships of students are included rather than the content of what the students should learn, in line with the 21st Century Skills education programme. Former precepts and subject boundaries are thus doomed to fall. The skills that students of the future need are no longer just subject-specific but cognitive and practical, social and emotional – something the Ludvigsen Committee believes must be of consequence for how the school day is designed. The proposals for more in-depth learning and interdisciplinary schooling stem from this mindset. The Ludvigsen Committee report is regarded as one, if not *the* most important supporting document for the preparation of *Report to the Storting 28 Subjects – Specialisation – Understanding: A renewal of the Knowledge Promotion Reform*, which was launched in spring 2016. A satisfied Ludvigsen recently noted in retrospect that the NOU he chaired and the report to the Storting that followed has 80–85 percent compliance.[52] And it states that "the Government [proposes] that three interdisciplinary subjects should be prioritised; democracy and citizenship, sustainable development and health and life skills. These are subjects that will influence social development". The interdisciplinary theme "health and life skills" is taken directly from the Ludvigsen Committee's recommendation and is rooted in the notion that students must be equipped for future social development, which will be characterised by both more responsibility and requirements to adapt and learn new things.

Ideological will

The last thing remaining in the contextualisation of life mastery is to ask whether it also contains a specific ideology but wrapped up and designed as an inviting, preventive public health measure aimed at children and young people, whereby the three P's – psychology, pedagogy and politics – apparently seem to merge into a higher unit. Although the Ludvigsen Committee can obviously be understood as a public inquiry that takes the 21st Century Skills educational programme seriously and even does what they have been asked, which is namely to investigate how Norwegian schools are currently equipped for the needs of the future, the report can also be read as an expression of something more than just an educational device, namely as a specific life or world view. A public inquiry that will say something about the School of the Future will necessarily have to accommodate a great deal of speculation and base its visions of the future on a series of both spoken and unspoken premises that are first and foremost expressions of contemporary currents of thought. Although the report is full of footnotes with reference to current research, it is composed by lecturers, educators and social economists and the content "is as secure as it can be".[53] According to the Chair of the Committee, the report also contains elements of a specific mindset that may be reminiscent of therapeutic learning, individualisation and neoliberalism. A common underlying denominator for all of these social ideologies is that characteristics of the individual – understood here as the individual student – are being used all the more as an explanation for why some are doing well in school and in life, while others are not doing quite so well.

Therapeutic learning

As far as I know, there is no existing, exact definition of *therapeutic education*, but two of the most important researchers, educators Kathryn Ecclestone and Dennis Hayes, provide the following post: "Therapeutic learning replaces traditional education with social impact directed at emotionally-schooled citizens who will be trained for emotional well-being".[54] They believe that in recent decades, such a tendency has made a name for itself in schools in Western countries such as the UK, the USA and Canada. If we look to the rhetoric of the Ludvigsen Committee, it is not difficult to find examples of how to emphasise that students' skills development both today and in the school of the future must be extended from traditional knowledge to apply to the whole person from a life cycle perspective: "Social and emotional skills that were previously seen as stable features of people can be developed and learned and have an impact on professional learning".[55] Psychology is also given precedence in the view of the Committee on learning and development in schools: "In the curricula, learning progression will be expressed by the central concepts, the methods and relationships in a subject that are linked to developmental and learning psychology".[56] The report also emphasises that students shall get assistance with their personal development and identity project: "The social mission of the school includes more than skills as goals in subjects. The school must also support the students' identity development, facilitate good interpersonal relationships and work systematically with the social environment at the school".[57] The tendency of the Committee to rely on psychology fits well with descriptions of the therapeutic education movement from other countries. In the book *The Education of Selves: How Psychology Transformed Students,* psychologist Jack Martin and social worker Ann-Marie McLellan provide the following outlines of this educational ideology:

> This book explores the role of scientific and professional psychology in transforming the ideal of student behaviour, experiences and goals in American and Canadian schools in the latter half of the 20th century. This was a time when psychological concepts, measurements, research and interventions related to the student's "self", gained great influence in school and classroom rhetoric and practices. As a consequence, educational objectives, policies and outcomes were increasingly directed towards the personal development of students as individuals, with high levels of self-esteem, self-image, belief in coping and self-regulation. The activities in the classroom were no longer just about assisting students in developing knowledge, skills and attitudes but also shaping their "psychological self".[58]

So, what is at stake here in this view that has already made a name for itself in countries such as the UK, the USA and Canada? The most critical voices see the growth of therapeutic impulse within the education system as a worrying expression of a time-sensitive self-centeredness in late modernity that has now reached the school. Perhaps the most influential critics, Ecclestone and Hayes, who were referred to previously, open their own book, bearing the alarming title *The Dangerous Rise of Therapeutic Education,* with a quote by a troubled history teacher in London: "You know that something has changed when young people want to learn more about themselves than about the world".[59] In my view, the critic's warning about selfishness, egoism or narcissism linked to therapeutic education is based on a somewhat simplified understanding of the processes of change that lead to the prevalence of the movement. Instead, it is possible to understand this educational movement as a response to historical societal changes, where young people are expected to create and manage themselves in a more radical way than did previous generations. But the psychological solutions prescribed by the therapeutic education movement are not necessarily the right social medicine and at worst, may have a reinforcing rather than reversing effect on these features of development.

Individualisation

One of the most important human consequences of the development of modernity is individualisation. Traditional social coexistence is broken down because civil, political and social rights, paid employment, education and increased demand for mobility in working life are oriented towards the individual and no longer aligned with groups. The extent to which this happens is so comprehensive that for the first time in history, the individual has become the fundamental unit of societal reproduction. Sociologist Ulrich Beck emphasises how individualisation guarantees free movement and opportunities to develop that were previously reserved for the few.[60] At the same time, individualisation means that the individual is increasingly being held accountable for their choices and the outcomes of these. The distinction between external events beyond our control and our ability to cope with them through individual mastery that was previously so clear is no longer as clear. One of Beck's examples is the unemployment in West Germany in the 1980s, which was increasingly less talked about as a national crisis but rather as an individual problem. The tendency in Western societies is for the individual to be asked to find biographical solutions to structural crises. Thus, individualisation also weakens class awareness of a common cause and fragments collective experiences into individual problems or "challenges", in which you are invited to break the bonds that are holding you down. Beck also describes individualisation as institutionalised, as social institutions force everyone to relate their circumstances to themselves and their lives as individualists.

In the 21st century, there is often talk about the new individualism as a further cementing of these features. In the book *The New Individualism: The Emotional Costs of Globalization*, by sociologists Anthony Elliott and Charles Lemert, the authors solder together both opportunities and pitfalls for the generation that is growing up today.[61] The most distinct feature of the new individualism is that seemingly opposite aspects emerge together: Freedom and alienation are both the result of the social context that shaped and bonded the lives of previous generations having in many ways disappeared. And the cure is everything from self-help manuals to therapy to cosmetic surgery and changes of identity. People must be expected to produce their own context to a greater extent; to create a life, a self-project that is deeply rooted, both as a social norm and cultural imperative. Individual solutions to globalised risks and political problems now become the motto of contemporary times.

If we look to the Norwegian school, it is also not unaffected by this new individualised worldview. In his main work, *Primary School as the Builder of a Nation* pedagogue, Alfred Oftedal Telhaug describes how since the interwar period progressive education has been eager for the work of learning to be transferred to the pupils themselves to a greater extent. But it wasn't until the 2000s that he believed this became a reality: "It is justified to speak of a more individualised student role".[62] In the account of the Norwegian school after the millennium, Telhaug also highlights tendencies that point to the Ludvigsen Committee:

> Unit thinking must give way so that students who are already in primary school are trained for a life in an electoral society that will give them great opportunities to manage their own lives as adults. They must be trained for an adult life based on self-discipline. In schools, greater responsibility for their own learning must therefore be taken and therefore, they must be given greater freedom or right to an individualised life.[63]

In the Ludvigsen Committee report on the skills that the school of the future must offer, it is precisely the individualisation that makes public health, life mastery and self-regulated learning necessary:

> Given an increased individualisation of society and the great access to information, the Committee considers skills that are related to making responsible choices in your own life to be important. Knowledge of your own body and health, including mental health, lifestyle, personal finances and consumption are areas in which a strengthening in school is necessary. The Commission recommends that emphasis be placed on a health and life skills perspective in subjects where relevant and appropriate.[64]

This section does not immediately seem to be more controversial; it simply seems to take the necessary consequences of the increased demands of individualisation to the students. At the same time, it is worth noting how Beck, who is the Ludvigsen Committee reference here, points out that individualisation is driven by both historical developments and an ongoing political ideology in the West that calls for more responsibility on the part of individuals, especially if things go badly. Ergo, it is possible to envision another political ideology that seeks to slow individualisation rather than reinforce it. Sociologist, Torben Hviid Nielsen has also commented on how contemporary diagnoses such as individualisation can also seem self-reinforcing:

> If individuals understand the challenges of their own life in the concepts of contemporary diagnosis, the diagnoses can therefore be made in a kind of double reflexivity – both becoming a self-imposed burden and assuming the character of a self-fulfilling prophecy.[65]

And that is why the Ludvigsen Committee solution, which consists of public health, life mastery and self-regulated learning, is far from unproblematic but rather an expression of a debatable worldview.

Neoliberalism

Between 1978 and 1979, philosopher Michel Foucault gave a lecture series at the Collège de France[66] in which he introduced the concept of *governmentality*, which has attempted to translate into Norwegian in a rendition that does not quite solder the particular fusion between the consciousness of the individual and the State guidelines in the West to which Foucault referred and as the English translation and French original (*gouvernementalité*) measure. Foucault referred to this as the governance of governance, which included the subtle ways in which advanced, liberal governments in the West control their citizens through a series of empowering approaches such as autonomy, self-actualisation, self-regulation and self-esteem. Not least in terms of education and health policy. These self-technologies, as Foucault calls them effectively enable individuals to control themselves and that they can be healthy citizens, so that the police, the judge and the doctor do not have to get involved. *Governmentality* is meant to show how neoliberal governance is not just ideological rhetoric or a series of political-economic reforms but a political project that seeks to establish a social reality that neoliberalism claims is already a reality.[67] Perhaps the best single illustration of this political project is from an interview with former Conservative Prime Minister of Britain Margaret Thatcher, in the women's magazine, *Woman's Own* in 1987 in which Thatcher rejects that there is such a thing as a society, when journalist Douglas Keay asks her what has gone wrong in Britain in recent years with rising divorce rates, abortion rates and episodes of violence:

> I think we've gone through a period in which far too many children and adults have developed an understanding of "I have a problem, it's the government's job to deal with it!' or "I have a problem, I have to get financial support to deal with it!' or "I'm homeless, the State has to house me!' and so they project their problems onto society and who is society? There's no such thing! There are individual men and women and there are families.[68]

Here, the emphasis is placed on the responsibility to fend for yourself in terms of not being misunderstood. However, that is not entirely true, because the quote "There is no such thing as a society" has often been rendered as if Thatcher is advocating an ultraliberalism or pure individualism here,[69] adding in subsequent parts of the interview that we all have a duty to care about ourselves and our neighbour. This must be understood to mean that something the size of society cannot exist without a minimum number of people who are willing to take responsibility and do their duty. At the same time, it is inevitable that in the same passage, Thatcher also announces a deep concern that welfare dependence will spread in the population: "But what is the point of working? I can get just as much on unemployment benefits!" she mocks.[70]

This is not to say that the Solberg government in Norway in 2020 is a blueprint. It is still officially stated that public health is largely determined by social conditions outside the individual and that it is the responsibility of the authorities, but the trend in recent years can reasonably be characterised as neoliberal in the sense of increased individualisation and accountability. In *The Public Health Report – Coping and Opportunities*, there is even an expressed concern about the possible protective effect of the welfare society and a similar argument for renewal, which may be reminiscent of Thatcher's fears but in somewhat softer objections:

> This means that we must both strengthen the individual's ability to cope and at the same time make the good choices easy. We must not incapacitate but create conditions so that we can be in control in our own lives. We must develop the welfare society so that it is adapted to the needs of the individual and so that we all have the opportunity to develop the best in us. This requires a renewal that means that individuals emerge from the masses – that we create a welfare society that does not protect but stimulates.[71]

In particular, the phrase "individuals emerge from the masses" illustrates that it is the individual who has become the primary reference point and not society but customarily, rhetorically packaged as an invitation to the reader to step out of anonymity. However, a widespread misconception of Foucault is that the neoliberal form of government is the result of a conspiratorial plot or a skewed policy that only serves the economic elite. Rather, his point was that it represents a historic change in the way one governs, where it is no longer a matter of ruling over countries and populations but making sure that the individual citizens rule over themselves. Whether this development is unfortunate is another matter. At the same time, there is little doubt that this shift that seeks to establish a more individual-oriented framework of reference for the policy involves greater responsibility for the individual and the requirement to manage your own life and health. In 1980, economist Robert Crawford launched the concept of healthism to describe the tendency to put health and disease in individual-oriented categories, where the solutions are found at the same level.[72] And while the public health report now contains words stating that "everyone has the opportunity to develop the best in us", the economic disparities in the population are also increasing.

You are supposed to regulate yourself

Is there a basis for considering the Ludvigsen Committee and life mastery in school as a further step towards the individual student managing or regulating themselves? The Ludvigsen Committee report on *The School of the Future* is primarily rooted in the visions of the international 21st Century Skills movement. Here, the idea is that in the working life of the future you must adapt to a greater extent therefore, the Committee is particularly concerned with developing the ability of the individual student to learn. Under the four skills areas that together will renew the content of the school, the compulsory "subject-specific skills" innovation in introduced in accordance with "skills in learning":

> That students can reflect on the purpose of what they learn, what they have learned and how they learn is called metacognition. Students who develop a conscious relationship with their own learning, who learn about learning and think about how they learn are better equipped to solve problems in a reflective way, alone and with others. Being able to use different strategies for planning, implementing and assessing your own learning and work processes is one part of this. That the students in collaboration with teachers and fellow students learn to take the initiative and work purposefully to learn and learn to regulate their own thinking and their own actions and feelings is called self-regulation. The Committee recommends that an emphasis is placed on metacognition and self-regulated learning in all subjects.[73]

The influence of the cognitive learning theory, which focuses on the thinking activities of young people in learning, is obvious here. Not least, this applies to the two key concepts of metacognition and self-regulation, which the Ludvigsen Committee considers so important that it recommends emphasising these in all subjects. The visions presented by the Ludvigsen Committee for *The School of the Future* attracted both enthusiasm and debate in the Norwegian public. However, much of the debate was on the concept of in-depth learning and subsequent space-saving controversial cuts in what Norwegian students should now learn in subjects such as Norwegian and history.[74] However, the fact that the two psychological concepts of metacognition and self-regulation suddenly gained a whole new rea of application went relatively unnoticed. These two related concepts originated in the 1960s and 1970s in the psychology laboratories of one of the most prestigious universities in the world – Stanford University in the heart of Silicon Valley. How have they been able to expand to become key reference points and scientific footnotes in a public report on the school of the future in Norway half a century later?

Metacognition

Metacognition can be defined as knowledge and insight into one's own thought processes. The term can be traced back to 1970s and is often credited to John Flavell, professor emeritus in developmental psychology at Stanford University in California. In a widely cited article, *"Metacognition and Cognitive Monitoring"* from 1979, Flavell refers to studies of preschoolers and schoolchildren who were given a task of remembering a variety of objects and letting them know when they were sure they could remember them.[75] As a rule, schoolchildren manage this while preschoolers usually do not – they say they are ready when really they are not. Similarly, preschoolers often fail on tasks in which they are supposed to reveal that the instructions they are given are incorrect and they claim they manage to follow them, when in fact it's impossible. Such coincidental findings led Flavell to draw the conclusion that young children have limited knowledge and awareness of their cognitive processes – what he calls metacognition – as children monitor their own memory, understanding and other cognitive activity only to a small extent. Flavell therefore aimed to develop a model of metacognition as a central element of all learning, as metacognition is believed to play an important role in oral communication, argumentation, comprehension, reading, writing, language acquisition, attention, memory, problem solving, social cognition, self-control and self-instruction. The implications for education were numerous, and Flavell pointed to experiments with mentally disabled children who using metacognitive strategies, learned to remember orders. Another study tested how children can become more effective readers by continuously monitoring their own comprehension as they read. Flavell concludes with a promising vision that in addition to teaching children to understand and learn better in the school situation, metacognition will be able one day to teach both children and adults to make wise and thoughtful life decisions: "I am entirely convinced that there is far too little and not too much cognitive monitoring in this world".[76] Metacognition has already been in fashion in education for decades, long before the Ludvigsen Committee embraced it. In a review article that is more than 20 years old, Jennifer Livingston refers to metacognition as "one of the last fashionable words in educational psychology".[77]

Self-regulation

Self-regulation can be defined as "exercising control over action, thought and emotions in line with what is in the best interests of the person in the long run".[78] It is common to argue that unlike self-control – which deals exclusively with resisting impulses and temptations in the immediate present – self-regulation can include observing oneself over time and one's own values and desires. Self-regulation is aimed at longer-term goals ("I want to lose weight") and allows us to cope with situations where the goal is threatened ("I fancy this chocolate now but don't eat it because I have a long-term goal of losing weight"). Like metacognition, self-regulation has seemingly gained a broad impact in recent concerns about children's development. Norway is not an exception in this respect.

Before the Ludvigsen Committee, several key players have also believed that self-regulation is such an important skill in today's society that it should be included even before starting school. One of them is the Learning Environment Centre at the University of Stavanger, which is responsible for the NFR-supported project *School Ready!* In an interview, project leader and professor of educational psychology Ingunn Størksen emphasises that "self-regulation is essential for learning and social adaptation in the first stages of school and also from a life cycle perspective. Especially important for self-regulation is what happens at the ages of three to five years".[79] Størksen refers to self-regulation as nothing less than the foundation for all later development and learning. At preschool ages, one has a unique window to learn self-regulation, she claims. In this respect, it should be added that one of the members of the Ludvigsen Committee Professor of Economics Mari Rege is the project manager, along with Størksen, for the *Agder Project*, which is testing a new educational programme in kindergartens and daycare facilities in Agder – so-called play-based learning – in which the core areas are social competence, language, mathematics and self-regulation. From the podium at the NHO annual conference in 2014, Rege even advocated starting to learn in kindergartens and daycare facilities, as it will be socioeconomically profitable.[80]

The notion that people should control their will and impose discipline on themselves is far from new. From ancient times, we have Homer's accounts of Odysseus' ability to withstand ordeals, for example when he encounters the alluring song of the sirens. Odysseus ties himself to the mast and equips the crew with wax in their ears. A classic case of self-regulation strategies in which precautions are taken and do not rely on pure and sheer willpower to resist. Moreover, the Christian account of creation illustrates how things develop when man's control over himself does not work: Adam and Eve are cast out of the Garden of Eden.

In our time, the notion of self-regulation is particularly associated with a now classic psychological experiment: Walter Mischel's marshmallow experiment. The Ludvigsen Committee does not mention the experiment explicitly in the report itself but refers to it in the footnotes as supporting precisely the perception that self-regulation has an impact on both students' learning in school and later mastery of their own lives. In reality, the Marshmallow experiment is essentially about a series of experiments with various rewards, the first of which was conducted as early as 1958 and later followed up in different variations at Stanford University in the USA throughout the 1960s, 1970s and 1980s. The pilot study took place in the Caribbean island state of Trinidad and Tobago, where Mischel happened to be located in connection with the socioanthropological fieldwork of his wife, Frances Mischel.[81] He became aware of a widespread perception that applied to the two largest ethnic groups: Ancestors of slaves from the African continent and the descendants of Indian migrant workers from the 1840s. The African inhabitants were perceived primarily as impulsive and pleasure-oriented while those born in India were perceived as more plan- and duty-oriented. Mischel decided to test the stereotype on 53 boys and girls aged seven to nine years. The children were given the choice between a small one-cent sweet that they could eat right away or a more exclusive sweet for ten cents that they had to wait a week to eat. Mischel found an essential difference between the two groups, although it is not quite as obvious as the prejudice would suggest. Of the ethnic Indian group, 67 per cent of the children chose to wait, as opposed to just 38 per cent of children from the ethnic African group. Less noticeable is that Mischel also investigated whether the children had a father present or not. Perhaps because the test leader himself was male, Mischel believed that their own experiences of waiting for rewards from a male person could affect the result. But as there was only one fatherless child in the Indian group, this measurement was not undertaken for them. Of the 13 children of ethnic African descent who wanted to wait for the more precious sweet, all had a father present, while of the 22 who chose the immediate reward, twelve had a father living at home and ten did not. I emphasise this little-noticed aspect here because a later replication should point to related explanations. After this pilot experiment, Mischel returned to Stanford University for a series of studies throughout the 1960s and 1970s that are later referred to only as the marshmallow experiment. In the study in which the marshmallow was first introduced, 90 children aged three years and six months to five years and five months are recruited from a kindergarten/daycare facility for the children of students and staff at the university.[82] One by one, they are offered the chance to double their reward if they manage to wait to eat the marshmallow until the experiment leader returns. Some children are impulsive and gobble it up as soon as he disappears out the door, some give in to the temptation after a few minutes. Some children exhibit cunning by taking a bite and turning it upside down to try to hide it. While one group of children manage to wait 15 minutes and then receive the reward in the form of another marshmallow. These children often use advanced diversion strategies such as playing in another part of the room, counting to themselves or lying down and relaxing – all to divert attention from the object of desire.

So what was it about these discoveries that made them so famous? Actually, not so much. Mischel gained recognition in the field of research on delayed reward and self-control for which he publishing the findings, but this was not further known publicly. It wasn't until the late 1980s that Mischel's research became widely known. Coincidentally, Mischel's daughter was a peer of many of the children from the original experiments and he was regularly told stories about them at the dinner table. He was therefore curious to test how they had turned out and decided to compare their development to the original results they got as four-year-olds. Mischel collected information about 90 children from parents and teachers and had them assess the academic performance and social functioning of the children. The results of the new investigation showed that those who managed best to wait patiently as young children consistently fared best as teenagers as well.[83] The adult individuals around these teenagers assessed them as generally more competent both at school and outside school, more verbal, rational, concentrated, systematic and resilient and better equipped to cope with challenges in life.

This is what made the marshmallow experiment known to the wider public. Psychologist Daniel Goleman helped highlight the ability to self-regulate as the foremost single factor for success in life alongside intelligence by linking it to his popular message about the importance of emotional intelligence (EQ).[84] As there is a consensus that intelligence is probably largely due to genes, which cannot be trained, the focus instead turned to self-regulation as an area in which one's own efforts could make a significant difference. Throughout the 1990s, 2000s and 2010s, the marshmallow experiment appears to be gaining increasing attention through government programmes, research dissemination, popular science and psychologically-oriented self-help literature. Mischel himself dates the surge in interest to the early 2000s when he bumped into children wearing t-shirts that read "Don't eat the marshmallow" and "I passed the marshmallow test". In the children's TV series *Sesame Street*, the Cookie Monster must learn to master his impulses. The 44th President of the USA, Barack Obama, is a prime example of the self-regulated man who selects the suit of the day in advance so as not to unnecessarily drain his reserve of will. He also reportedly enjoys seven almonds – never six or eight – every night. In 2016, when Brad Pitt and Angelina Jolie split up, Pitt accused Jolie of lacking a self-regulating mechanism in the legal dispute over custody of the children.[85] Self-regulation – whether you are capable of it to a great extent or not at all – seems to be becoming a new gold standard for how to assess people.

In Norway, the experiment in the 2010s was an eye-opener, for example in the many you-reports: "Sure, you can resist the temptations', and "Can your child resist this?"[86] The book *Willpower* by renowned psychologist Roy Baumeister and journalist John Tierney was translated into Norwegian in 2013, and on the cover of the Norwegian edition, a child stares intensely at a small pyramid of pink marshmallows. In 2014, Walter Mischel's own book, *The Marshmallow Test,* was published in Norwegian and featured a towering example of the spongy sweet on the cover. When Mischel was in Scandinavia to promote the book, it was only natural for him to appear in the largest media channels, such as in the leather chair in Fredrik Skavlan's *First & Last* and in an extended report in *A-magazine*. Because we increasingly encounter Mischel's marshmallow experiment – usually illustrated with pink and white spongy treats – it helps cement the importance of self-regulation. In this way, the experiment has also prepared the ground for the self-regulation's breakthrough in a Norwegian public, such when men and women like Størksen and Rege postulate that it is the sole possible solution for Norwegian children in kindergarten or daycare, or when the Ludvigsen Committee places credence in it in its official report. How could the marshmallow experiment become so popular, and why has it gone global only now, 50 years later? One hypothesis may be that self-regulation is an appropriate solution to the challenges under the banner of new individualism, namely that people today must create a life in the absence of the rules and prohibitions of the old world. Self-regulation appears to be an obvious answer at a time when according to the most optimistic representations, everyone has the freedom to do what they want and where everyone is competing under the same conditions. Furthermore, such rhetoric fits perfectly with the emphasis of the Ludvigsen Committee on developing the potential of the students as human beings. The underlying moral is apparently that those who succeed are those who have been dedicated and have not let themselves be distracted by too many temptations.

Perhaps it is therefore not so surprising that Baumeister – Mischel's heir apparent in self-regulation research today – and Tierney nevertheless state that improving willpower is simply the key to a better life and a well-suited explanation as to why so many of us do not live better lives:

> Baumeister and colleagues around the world have found that improving your willpower is the best path to a better life. They have acknowledged that most problems, personal or social are about a lack of self-control: excessive consumption and loans, impulsive acts of violence, under performance in school, procrastination behaviour in school, alcohol and substance abuse, unhealthy diet, lack of exercise, chronic anxiety, explosive anger.[87]

Self-control is seemingly perfect as a methodological individualistic explanation for complex social problems, even to the point of being substantiated by social psychology experiments. If only the current and future population learn to make use of the science of self-control, these problems will gradually diminish or disappear.

Don't eat the marshmallow yet!

The belief in self-regulation is apparently also strong in the Ludvigsen Committee, but in 2013, Celeste Kidd and colleagues published a study in the journal *Cognition* in which they recreated Mischel's original marshmallow experiment, demonstrating why the common explanatory models based on individual differences in self-control were inadequate.[88] Instead, they point to a characteristic of trust as central, as the experience of children in trusting the outside world seems to have a major impact on whether or not they want to

wait for something good. Kidd allowed the children to go through two different courses before they were tested. One group, consisting of 14 children aged
three to five years were exposed to an unpredictable learning environment,
while the other group of the same size and age were exposed to predictable
conditions. In this one group, the children were told that they could get
a nicer tin of paint if they waited until the investigator returned from the
warehouse. The same course of events was repeated with a collection of
stickers. In both cases, the investigator kept to what he promised. In the second group, exactly the same thing was done but with a significant difference.
Both times, the investigator came back empty-handed, equipped only with
excuses such as "Sorry children, but the warehouse was empty". This pilot
study is designed to establish or undermine the trust the children have in the
investigator. Kidd then conduced a copy of Mischel's marshmallow experiment. On average, the group of children who had been subject to a credible
investigator managed to wait an average of twelve minutes and two seconds,
while the group in which the investigator could not be trusted waited on average only three minutes and two seconds. The researchers also saw whether the
children were able to wait until the maximum time of 15 minutes had passed
and in the group with a credible investigator, nine out of 14 children managed
to do so while in the group with an untrustworthy investigator, only one child
waited out the time.

> Our results do not show that self-control is irrelevant in explaining dif-
> ferences in the waiting times of the children in the original marshmallow
> study. However, they provide strong evidence that it is hasty to conclude
> that the observed difference [between children] and the long-term rela-
> tionship between waiting times and later outcomes in life are due to dif-
> ferences in the individual capacity for self-control. Instead, an unreliable
> worldview, in addition to self-control, may be causally associated with
> later outcomes in life, as is already suggested a number of existing facts.[89]

Kidd reasoned that what you consider rational behaviour in a particular situation is probably influenced by your past experiences. The article has also
been appropriately named "*Rational snacking*", because if you grow up in a
crowded orphanage with a lot of older children and do not always have immediate access to adult individuals, eating the sweet as quickly as possible may
be a good strategy because you can never know for sure if someone bigger
and stronger will try to take it away from you. On the other hand, children
who come from resourceful homes characterised by predictability have often
gained experience by making bets with their parents not to eat sweets with
the aim of strengthening their motivation and willpower. Broken promises
or possessions that disappear occur so rarely here that children will resort to
crying if that should happen. While in the first upbringing environment, it may
be part of everyday life. The popular notion that willpower and self-control

are readily accessible and something everyone can train to do may not be so obvious anymore, as children's assumptions and experiences from early in life give them vastly different starting points. Thus, the marshmallow experiment illustrates the possibilities and limitations of self-regulation.

The story of the marshmallow experiment also shows how tempting it can be to give the different outcomes of scientific experiments seemingly neutral explanations about individual differences based on psychological variables. The ability to self-control in given situations can be explained by both individual and environmental factors, but the impulse to explain outcomes in life with personal characteristics seems to be strong. It is remarkable how psychological concepts such as self-control and self-regulation are given precedence over a more relational concept such as trust. And if you want to keep talking about self-regulation, you should at least always do so with the knowledge that children do not always grow up in stable home environments or have fairly predictable and meaningful existences. As a comment on the revised marshmallow experiment points out: "Kidd's work suggests that making children better at waiting – in the laboratory and in life in general – is about convincing them that there is something worth waiting for".[90] Talking about self-regulation without talking about the content of children's lives becomes not only bland but also ideological, as it creates the impression that everyone gets what they deserve in life. In fact, when confronted with the revision of the experiment, Mischel himself also lamented that in the reception there has been a tendency to extract what is most relevant to an individualistic concept of self-control.[91] While the more complex background variables in which Mischel also already took an interest in the pilot study in Trinidad and Tobago, such as whether children came from a home with or without a father present, have not been recounted. This perhaps only illustrates how a scientific experiment such as this, when it is taken up in culture, will necessarily always undergo a filtering based on the dominant assessment of values. No research is completely neutral – science is always in a relationship with society and the culture of which it is a part. The Ludvigsen Committee report does not mention Kidd's revisions and reservations anywhere.

Another recent replication of the Marshmallow experiment has emerged but with 900 children – ten times as many children as in the original experiment conducted by Mischel – and this also showed that controlling for socioeconomic differences explained the results.[92] Like Kidd, the researchers here point out how children from more affluent families can reasonably expect to receive an even more valuable reward if they behave well and refrain from temptation, while for poorer families, sweets come at more uneven intervals and perhaps enjoying food from McDonald's or sweets are the most exclusive benefits the children are used to.

The Ludvigsen Committee's emphasis on lifelong learning offers alluring promises of endless possibilities rather than the more entrenched views of the students in the past. At the same time, the students must bear the responsibility for any restrictions on change and growth themselves. This is also largely the experience of self-regulation from other countries. Based on experiences from the USA and Canada, Martin and McLellan have warned that without a clear distinction between self-regulation and the regulation of a student's behaviour or learning by a teacher or psychologist, the only thing that changes under the therapeutic philosophy of education is a redistribution of responsibility for learning – from the experts to the students themselves.[93] In defence of the Ludvigsen Committee, it must be added that they also reflect on this danger when they concede that concepts such as responsibility for own learning from previous school reforms, such as Reform 94 and Reform 97, probably meant that responsibility was shifted more to the student even though this was not the intention. The Committee emphasises that even if you want to train students to work more independently, it is still the school and the teachers who are responsible for facilitating the student learning processes.[94] But the question is whether the concession is enough to prevent further reinforcement of the tendencies brought about by the major reforms in Norwegian schools in the 1990s.

And quite rightly in several places in the report, the Committee is no stranger to taking a view according to which the individual has a greater responsibility for himself/herself than before. This is linked to increasing health challenges such as obesity and mental illness and also to increased individualisation, where the Committee largely accepts its consequences as an undisputed premise: "In addition, individualisation as a feature of social development gives relevance to student motivation and coping experience related to taking responsibility for their own lives".[95] NOU reports have a neutral intent but in reality they exercise influence using neutrality as a tool. No matter how and to what extent they use science as a source, such reports will always lean on certain interests, priorities and values. But they prefer to try to convince us that issues and politics and facts and values are, and should be, separated. Thus, the Ludvigsen report is a reminder that this does not work as its favourite educational psychology words – metacognition and self-regulation – represent the preferred solutions under the new individualism in the form of broad-appeal psychological approaches, where of course there is a great temptation to apply them to themselves, their children or their students. But where do you find the self-regulation tool to resist this individualising and "psychologising" impulse? "You must govern yourself!" – this is what the title of a column by political scientists Iver B. Neumann and Ole Jacob Sending sounded like just over a decade ago.[96] Their decree played on the neo-liberal notion of the citizen as most self-governing as possible and is inspired precisely by Foucault's concept of *governmentality*, in which governance and mentality become one and the same project. "You must regulate yourself!" is how we might have to rephrase this today. While the neoliberalism of the 2000s was political science in its form, the influence of subjects such as psychology and behavioural science is clearer in the 2010s and 2020s. In this

48 *Life mastery in context*

sense, even if they are not always in line with the latest research, the Ludvigsen Committee recommendations are at least in line with the spirit of time.

Notes

1 Wilhelm Dilthey, "Avgrensning av åndsvitenskapene" [Demarcation of the intellectual sciences]", in the book, *Hermeneutisk lesebok* [*Hermeneutics and the Study of History*], ed. Sissel Lægreid and Torgeir Skogen (Oslo: Scandinavian Academic Press, 2014).
2 Per Halvorsen, "Tilpasser utdanningen til nye psykologroller [Adapting education to new psychology roles]", *The Norwegian Psychological Association* (2019, 28.2.), www.psykologforeningen.no/foreningen/aktuelt/aktuelt/tilpasser-utdanningen-til-nye-psykologroller.
3 Arne Holte, "Slik fremmer vi psykisk helse, forebygger psykiske lidelser og får en mer fornuftig samfunnskøkonomi [How we promote mental health, prevent psychological disorders and get more sensible social economics]", *Utposten: Journal of General and Social Medicine* no. 2 (2017), www.utposten.no/i/2017/2/utposten-2-2017b-457.
4 Geoffrey Rose, *The Strategy of Preventive Medicine* (Oxford: Oxford University Press, 1992).
5 Katherine L. Frohlich and Louise Potvin, "Transcending the known in public health practice", *American Journal of Public Health* 98, no. 2 (2008).
6 Ibid.
7 Jo C. Phelan and Bruce G. Link, "Controlling disease and creating disparities: A fundamental cause perspective", *Journals of Gerontology: SERIES* B 60B, No. Special Issue II (2005).
8 Frohlich and Potvin, "Transcending the known in public health practice."
9 Bruce G. Charlton, "A critique of Geoffrey Rose's population strategy for preventive medicine", *Journal of the Royal Society of Medicine* 88, no. 11 (1995).
10 Ibid., 609.
11 Geoffrey Rose, "Sick individuals and sick populations", *International Journal of Epidemiology* 14 (1985).
12 Lisbet Skregelid, "Generasjon prestasjon og kunsten å mestre livet [Generation achievement and the art of mastering life]", *University of Agder* (2018, 18.10.), www.uia.no/nyheter/generasjon-prestasjon-og-kunsten-aa-mestre-livet; Merete Lund Fasting, "Bevegelse, lek og friluftsliv kan bidra til livsmestring [Movement, play and outdoor activities can contribute to life mastery]", *Utdanningsnytt* (2020, 18.3.), www.utdanningsnytt.no/livsmestring-merete-lund-fasting-utelek/bevegelse-lek-og-friluftsliv-kan-bidra-til-livsmestring/235397.
13 Claire Fox, *I Find That Offensive!* (London: Biteback, 2016); Theodore Dalrymple, *Admirable Evasions: How Psychology Undermines Morality* (New York: Encounter Books, 2015).
14 Ole Jacob Madsen, "Inger velger å bli syke. Men kulturell påvirkning forekommer [No one chooses to get sick: But cultural influence is present]", *Aftenposten* (2020, 11.2.), www.aftenposten.no/viten/i/Jo4oo8/ingen-velger-aa-bli-syke-men-kulturell-paavirkning-forekommer-ole-jacob-madsen?
15 Svend Brinkmann et al., "Diagnosekultur – et analytisk perspektiv på psykiatriske diagnoser I samtiden [Diagnostic culture: An analytical perspective on psychiatric diagnoses in the present]", *Journal of the Norwegian Psychology Association* 51, no. 9 (2014).
16 Ole Jacob Madsen, *The Therapeutic Turn* (London: Routledge, 2014).
17 Anders Bakken, *Ungdata 2019. Nasjonale resultater* [*Ungdata 2019: National Results*], NOVA Report 9/19 (Oslo: NOVA, OsloMet, 2019).

Life mastery in context 49

18 George A. Miller, "Psychology as a means of promoting human welfare", *American Psychologist* 24, no. 12 (1969).
19 Gunnar C. Aakvaag, "Inger slipper unna psykologien, men det er lov å prøve [No one escapes psychology but it is allowed to try]", *Morgenbladet* (2019, 29.11.), https://morgenbladet.no/ideer/2019/11/ingen-slipper-unna-psykologien-men-det-er-lov-prove-skriver-gunnar-c-aakvaag.
20 Per Halvorsen, "-Ikke fred uten psykologi [-No peace without psychology]", *Norwegian Psychology Association* (2011, 6.9.), http://psykologforeningen.no/Foreningen/Nyheter-og-aktuelt/Aktuelt/Ikke-fred-uten-psykologi/%28language%29/nor-NO.
21 Miller, "Psychology as a means of promoting human welfare", 1064.
22 The Norwegian Psychology Association, "Prinsipprogram [Principles programme]", *The Norwegian Psychology Association* (2010), www.psykologforeningen.no/foreningen/vedtekter-og-retningslinjer/prinsipprogram.
23 The Norwegian Psychology Association et al., *Boken som mangler [The Book That Is Missing]* (2015), www.psykologforeningen.no/foreningen/nyheter-og-kommentarer/aktuelt/krever-psykologi-i-skolen#opprop.
24 Ibid.
25 Emil André Erstad, "KrFU vil ta et oppgjør med prestasjonssamfunnet [Young Christian Democrats will take a stand against the achievement society]", *Ny Tid* (2015, 5.5.), www.nytid.no/krfu-vil-ta-oppgjor-med-prestasjonssamfunnet-2/.
26 Ibid., sec. 3.
27 Ibid., sec. 2.
28 Ibid., sec. 3.
29 For example, see Hartmut Rosa, *Fremmedgørelse och acceleration [Alienation and Acceleration]* (Copenhagen: Hans Reitzel, 2014).
30 Merete Glorvingen, "Lisa Maria Hareides tøffe høst [Lisa Maria Hareide's tough autumn]", *Kvinner & Klær* (2019), www.kk.no/livet/lisa-maria-hareides-toffe-host/70491258.
31 Kjell Ingolf Ropstad, "-Ingen skal kunne si at jeg var stille da de trengte meg [-No one should be able to say that I was quiet when they needed me]", *Christian Democratic Party* (2019, 28.4.), www.krf.no/nyheter/nyheter-fra-krf/-ingen-skal-kunne-si-at-jeg-var-stille-da-de-trengte-meg/.
32 The Bible, *The Bible: Authorized King James Version* (Oxford: Oxford University Press, 2008), Mark 6.34.
33 The Lutheran Confessional Church, "Som sauer uten hyrde [Like sheep without a shepherd]", *The Lutheran Confessional Church* (2003), www.luthersk-kirke.no/lbk-luthersk-kirke.no/andakt17-2003.htm.
34 Daniel Sæbjørnsen, "Generasjon prestasjon trenger å ledes til liv [Generation achievement needs to be brought to life]", *Faith & Media* (2019, 13.11), https://troogmedier.no/generasjon-prestasjon-trenger-a-ledes-til-liv/.
35 Margunn Serigstad Dahle, "'Sykt perfekt' speglar presset [Perfectly sick' reflects the pressure]", *Vårt Land* (2016, 13.1.), www.vl.no/sykt-perfekt-speglar-presset-1.674304?paywall=true.
36 Ole Martin Moen, "Fremtidsskolen [The school of the future]", *Dagbladet* (2018, 12.2.), www.dagbladet.no/kultur/fremtidsskolen/69443837, dec. 50.
37 Ibid.
38 Stortinget, "Stortinget – Møte tirsdag den 12. april 2016 kl. 10 [Stortinget: Meeting on Tuesday 12 April 2016 at 10]" (2016, 12.4.), www.stortinget.no/nn/Saker-og-publikasjoner/publikasjonar/Referat/Stortinget/2015-2016/160412/5/, 4:27:02.
39 Ibid., 4:30:27.
40 Ibid., 4:31:31.
41 Ibid., 4:43:28.

42 Ibid., 4:45:40.
43 Ibid., 4:46:50.
44 Ibid., 4:50:21.
45 Report to the Storting, Report St. 6, *Tett på – tidlig innsats og inkluderende fellesskap i barnehage, skole og SFO* [*Close: Early Intervention and Inclusive Communities in Kindergarten and Daycare Facilities, Schools and SFO*], Ministry of Education and Research (Oslo, 2019–2020), 12.
46 Jan Tore Sanner, "Elevene skal lære mer om psykisk helse og livsmestring i skolen [Students will learn more about mental health and life mastery in school]", *Aftenposten* (2019, 19.5.), www.aftenposten.no/meninger/debatt/i/y3xVpR/elevene-skal-laere-mer-om-psykisk-helse-og-livsmestring-i-skolen-jan-tore-sanner, avs. 14.
47 Stine Vik, "Tidlig innsats og barnehagen som forebyggingsarena [Early intervention and kindergarten and daycare facilities as a prevention arena]", in *Kindergarten and Daycare Facilities as a Community Institution*, ed. Solveig Østrem (Oslo: Cappelen Akademisk, 2018), 143.
48 Jon Kaurel, *Tidlig innsats i utdanningspolitikken – motiver, mål og motsetninger* [*Early Intervention in Education Policy: Motives, Goals and Contradictions*] (Oslo: Education Association, 2018), 4.
49 NOU 2014:7: *Elevenes læring i fremtidens skole* [*Student Learning in the School of the Future*], Ministry of Education and Research (Oslo: The Norwegian Government Security and Service Organisation, 2014).
50 The National Commission on Excellence in Education, *A Nation at Risk: The Imperative for Educational Reform* (Washington, DC: The National Commission on Excellence in Education, 1983), 10.
51 World Economic Forum, *New Vision for Education* (Geneva: World Economic Forum, 2015).
52 Lina Christensen, "Forskernes politiske fortrinn [The political advantage of researchers]", *Forskerforum* 52, no. 4 (2020): 23.
53 Ibid.
54 Ecclestone and Hayes, *The Dangerous Rise of Therapeutic Education*, xiii.
55 NOU 2015:8: *Fremtidens skole: Fornyelse av fag og kompetanser* [*The School of the Future: Renewal of Subjects and Skills*], Ministry of Education and Research (Oslo, 2015), 20.
56 Ibid., 11.
57 Ibid., 9.
58 Jack Martin and Ann-Marie McLellan, *The Education of Selves: How Psychology Transformed Students* (New York: Oxford University Press, 2013).
59 Ecclestone and Hayes, *The Dangerous Rise of Therapeutic Education*, viii.
60 Ulrich Beck, *Risk Society: Towards a New Modernity* (London: Sage, 1992).
61 Anthony Elliott and Charles Lemert, *The New Individualism: The Emotional Costs of Globalization* (Rev. Ed.) (New York: Routledge, 2009).
62 Alfred Oftedal Telhaug, *Grunnskolen som nasjonsbygger* [*Primary School the Builder of a Nation*] (Oslo: Abstrakt forlag, 2003), 415.
63 Ibid., 416.
64 NOU 2015:8: *Fremtidens skole: Fornyelse av fag og kompetanser* [*The School of the Future: Renewal of Subjects and Skills*], 50–2.
65 Torben Hviid Nielsen, "De 'frisatte'. Om individualisering og identitet i nyere samtidsdiagnoser [The 'freed': On individualisation and identity in recent contemporary diagnoses]", in *Klassebilder: Ulikheter og sosial mobilitet i Norge* [*Class Photos: Inequalities and Social Mobility in Norway*], ed. Kenneth Dahlgren and Jørn Ljunggren (Oslo: Universitetsforlaget, 2010).
66 Michel Foucault, *Security, Territory, Population: Lectures at the Collège de France, 1977–78* (Basingstoke: Palgrave Macmillan, 2007).

67 Thomas Lemke, "The birth of bio-politics: Michel Foucault's lecture at the Collège de France on neo-liberal governmentality", *Economy and Society* 30, no. 2 (2001).
68 Douglas Keay, "Interview for *Woman's Own* ('No such thing as society')" (1987), www.margaretthatcher.org/document/106689, 28–9.
69 Pål Mykkeltveit, "Det er galt å tro at konservativ politikk mister relevans i krisetid [It is wrong to think that conservative politics loses relevance in times of crisis]", *Minerva* (2020, 31.3.), www.minervanett.no/boris-johnson-konservatisme-koronavirus/det-er-galt-a-tro-at-konservativ-politikk-mister-relevans-i-krisetider/356100.
70 Keay, "Interview for *Woman's Own* ('No such thing as society')", 30.
71 Report to the Storting, Report St. 19, *Folkehelsemeldingen. Mestring og muligheter [Public Health Report: Coping and Opportunities]*, 12.
72 Robert Crawford, "Healthism and the medicalization of everyday life", *International Journal of Health Services* 10, no. 3 (1980).
73 NOU 2015:8: *Fremtidens skole: Fornyelse av fag og kompetanser [The School of the Future: Renewal of Subjects and Skills]*, 10.
74 See inter alia, Dag Eivind Undheim Larsen, "Pedagoger på dypt vann [Educators in deep water]", *Klassekampen* (2018, 8.12.), www.klassekampen.no/article/20181208/ARTICLE/181209971; Inger Merete Hobbelstad, "Neste gang du hører Høyre-folk snakke om å verne norsk kultur, må du le. På deres vakt skamferes norskfaget [The next time you hear Conservative people talk about protecting Norwegian culture, you might laugh: On their watch, the subject of Norwegian is mutilated], *Dagbladet* (2018, 25.3), www.dagbladet.no/kultur/neste-gang-du-horer-hoyre-folk-snakke-om-a-verne-norsk-kultur-ma-du-le-pa-deres-vakt-skamferes-norskfaget/69582172.
75 John H. Flavell, "Metacognition and cognitive monitoring: A new area of cognitive-developmental inquiry", *American Psychologist* 34, no. 10 (1979).
76 Ibid., 910.
77 Jennifer A. Livingston, "Metacognition: An overview" (1997), https://eric.ed.gov/?id=ED474273, sec. 1.
78 Frode Svartdal, "Selvregulering [Self-regulation]", *Store norske leksikon* (2014), https://snl.no/selvregulering.
79 Siw Ellen Jakobsen, "Selvregulering er grunnmuren for læring [Self-regulation is the foundation for learning]", *forskning.no* (2015, 25.1.), http://forskning.no/barn-og-ungdom-psykologi/2015/01/selvregulering-er-grunnmuren-laering, dec. 5.
80 Mari Rege, "Professor Mari Rege fra UiS på NHOs Årskonferanse 2014 [Professor Mari Rege from UiS at the NHO annual conference 2014]" (2014).
81 Walter Mischel, "Preference for delayed reinforcement: An experimental study of a cultural observation", *The Journal of Abnormal and Social Psychology* 56, no. 1 (1958).
82 Walter Mischel, Ebbe B. Ebbesen, and Antonette R. Zeiss, "Cognitive and attentional mechanisms in delay of gratification", *Journal of Personality and Social Psychology* 21, no. 2 (1972).
83 Walter Mischel, Yuichi Shoda, and Philip K. Peake, "The nature of adolescent competencies predicted by preschool delay of gratification", *Journal of Personality and Social Psychology* 54, no. 4 (1988).
84 Daniel Goleman, *Emotional Intelligence: Why It Can Matter More Than IQ* (London: Bloomsbury, 1996).
85 Chloe Melas, "Brad Pitt on Angelina Jolie in new court documents: 'She has no self-regulating mechanism'", *CNN* (2016, 22.12.), https://edition.cnn.com/2016/12/22/entertainment/brad-pitt-court-documents-custody/index.html.
86 Mari Valen Høihjelle, "Joda, du greier å stå imot fristelsene [Sure, you can resist temptation]", *ABC News* (2013, 9.6.), www.abcnyheter.no/livet/2013/06/09/175021/joda-du-greier-sta-imot-fristelsene; Camilla Tryggestad Visjø and Nils Bjåland,

"Can your child resist this?", *VG* (2013, 1.11), www.vg.no/nyheter/innenriks/i/L0x1J4/klarer-barnet-ditt-aa-motstaa-denne.
87 Roy F. Baumeister and John Tierney, *Willpower: Rediscovering the Greatest Human Strength* (New York: Penguin Press, 2011), 2.
88 Celeste Kidd, Holly Palmeri, and Richard N. Aslin, "Rational snacking: Young children's decision-making on the marshmallow task is moderated by beliefs about environmental reliability", *Cognition* 126, no. 1 (2013).
89 Ibid., 113.
90 Drake Bennett, "What does the Marshmallow Test actually test?", *Bloomsberg Businessweek* (2012), www.bloomberg.com/bw/articles/2012-10-17/what-does-the-marshmallow-test-actually-test., sec. 7.
91 Ibid.
92 Tyler W. Watts, Greg J. Duncan, and Haonan Quan, "Revisiting the marshmallow test: A conceptual replication investigating links between early delay of gratification and later outcomes", *Psychological Science* 29, no. 7 (2018).
93 Martin and McLellan, *The Education of Selves: How Psychology Transformed Students.*
94 NOU 2015:8: *Fremtidens skole: Fornyelse av fag og kompetanser* [*The School of the Future: Renewal of Subjects and Skills*].
95 Ibid., 52.
96 Iver B. Neumann and Ole Jacob Sending, "Du skal regjere deg selv [You shall govern yourself]", *Le Monde Diplomatique*, Nordic edition 2003.

3   Between risk and resilience

The whole subject renewal in which health and life skills are adopted as one of three interdisciplinary subjects in Norwegian schools is based on a specific understanding of the challenges encountered by children and young people that are often referred by the moniker *youth at risk*.[1] Typically here, adolescents are understood to be particularly exposed to problem behaviour such as substance abuse, dropping out of school, youth crime and mental illnesses such as anxiety and depression. And where the solution lies in facilitating young people is developing robustness. Or resilience, as it is called in professional speak. A psychological resilience that means that despite stress and strains, you can retain your mental strength and health.[2] This is often cited in justifications for the introduction of health and life skills. In the campaign *The Book That is Missing,* for example, Secretary General of the Council for Mental Health, Tove Gundersen, states: "We want robust kids who can meet the challenges of life and build good mental health".[3] In recent decades, a wealth of international research and commercial and government programmes aimed at youth at risk have emerged. In Norway we have Ungdata, which is a number of local youth surveys that are offered to all the municipalities and counties in the country. It is financed by the Norwegian Directorate of Health via an annual grant from the central government budget. Their annual surveys are frequently cited among the advocates of health and life skills in schools as a measure of how young Norwegian people really feel. Young people generally report that they are doing relatively well but at the same time are reporting increased mental health problems. However, it is often the latter that is reported in the media. The fact that the vast majority of people enjoy the life they live is not strictly a novelty. Thus, similar to young people in the risk tradition, Ungdata is otherwise in a tense relationship between being a source of knowledge and a source of concern that affects parents, teachers, health workers and politicians.

The fact that the adult generation looks at the younger generation with concern is far from new; it lies in the nature of the matter, or rather in human nature, not to approve differences in how *they* are and *we* are. Nevertheless, the adult unrest appears to be more pervasive and decisive than before. In

DOI: 10.4324/9781003372547-3

the yearbook *Students from 1909*, published on the 50th anniversary, you can read biographies and memoirs from a long life. One of these is head teacher Haakon Kristofersen, who has 49 years of professional experience from the primary schools in Oslo and Aker, who had just welcomed a third generation of students. Kristofersen apologises for the fact that the school places requirements on discipline, order and behaviour that are too low. The development is reportedly due to the misguided laissez-faire upbringing that is now being seen both at home and in the schools. Despite the moral decay, Kristofersen is still hopeful on behalf of the young:

> But even though today it seems that some of our magnificent Norwegian youth have lost a firm grip, I still believe that these youth problems will be solved without all the psychology. Of course we were filled with the desire to oppose and rebel and had a longing for freedom ourselves, which could often have strange outcomes, but see whether life, the great teacher, knew how to restrain us.[4]

The summary by Kristofersen of the teaching work over half a century provides insight into a mindset that seems to have almost run out with the sands of time. Here, he expresses a confidence that "life, the great teacher" has an inherently uplifting effect on the generation that is growing up and its shortcomings, and that recognising this prevents an undesirable psychologising of adolescent problems. The reasoning today seems to have been turned upside down: The psychology of our life world is total, and life mastery is considered necessary for as many young people as possible to be able to cope with life. Unlike head teacher Kristofersen, the supporters of life mastery lack the necessary confidence in the civilising effect of life in the transition from adolescent to adult. In a post in Aftenposten in 2020, psychologist Kari Halstensen, responsible for the Modum Bad *#psyktnormalt*, teaching programme in life skills, writes that focusing on young people's mental health in school is life-defining:

> At a challenging time when the pressure on the mental health of young people has increased, life mastery has gained its own place on the school timetable.
>
> It is not intended that each student has to identify their own symptoms but that safe adult voices should be given some extra time and space in which to teach safety – of course not through clinging to self-delivery but by displaying an honest picture of human life as a search to find the balance between the ordinary and the unique.
>
> Good mental health is about being one of all – and at the same time giving space to the uniqueness of your own personality. No one can find their way there alone.[5]

Understood as a paraphrasing of "No man is an island, whole and uncut in itself", few would disagree with the final point made by Halstensen. We get our identity through others. And in our relationships with others, we hold the lives of others in our hands.[6] But as this post is about life skills in school, it is not unreasonable to read it as if no one finds their way to a well-integrated identity and good mental health without being taught it. It must be able to be described as far more debatable.

Being young is hell

Life skills in school would never have been introduced without the perception that children and adolescents are facing challenges today that exceed those of previous generations. I have previously questioned whether this really is the case and have shown that many people today seem at least to be convinced that it is indeed the case.[7] Even His Majesty King Harald of Norway, in his New Year's address to the nation, soberly supports the idea that "young people today are facing so many more choices and so much more external influence and pressure than was the case only one to two generations ago".[8] And yes, there are some investigations and trends over time that can support this. In the Ungdata surveys, increasingly more young people are reporting having mental health problems. For girls, the number has increased throughout the 2010s and for the boys there has been an increase from 2015 onwards.[9] In lower secondary school, 22 percent of girls and eight percent of boys, and in upper secondary school, 31 percent of girls and twelve percent of boys report this. The most typical are stress-related symptoms. And unsurprisingly, young people themselves want life mastery to solve exactly that problem. "We have seen that what they [young people] have been most concerned about finding solutions to are different types of stress and pressure", said General Secretary Martin Ulvestad Østerdal of the National Council of Norway's Children and Youth Organisations during the presentation of the report *Life Skills in Schools* to then Minister of Education Torbjørn Røe Isaksen.[10] Grade pressure and achievement anxiety, time pressure and body pressure come out on top as the most frequent forms of unwanted pressure young people experience. In the Report to the Storting *Subject – Specialisation – Understanding – A renewal of the Knowledge Promotion Reform* in which health and life skills are adopted, the following objectives have also been included: "The school will contribute to equipping students for a society in which many young people experience different types of pressure".[11]

However, the paradox is that it is precisely the school itself that is cited as the foremost source of stress and pressure, especially among girls, where 45 percent find that it is a burden.[12] And while Steffen Handal, head of the Education Association, sees such results in the context of "an excessive belief in measurement, testing and competition as the path to learning and increased quality" in schools, Isaksen, minister of education at the time, seems less interested in talking about the content in school and instead points out that "more girls are negatively affected by life" and "pressure from the surrounding society".[13]

Viewed from the outside, it may seem strange that an arena identified as the foremost cause of stress and pressure is absolved. Also when we know that young people are already inclined to blame themselves: "But first and foremost, they blame themselves and think they need to be tougher or get better at coping with the stress. This is an unfair individualisation", says NOVA researcher Ingunn Eriksen after interviewing young people about their views on stress and pressure.[14]

In WHO's surveys of how 11-year-olds experience pressures related to school work, Norway admittedly comes out fairly low, in 37th place out of 41 European countries.[15] Thirteen percent of Norwegian girls and 12 percent of boys report that they experience pressure. When you ask 13-year-olds the same thing, Norway rises to 25th place, where the distribution is now 33 percent of girls and 28 percent of boys. Among 15-year-olds, Norway comes in at 15th place, with 66 percent of girls and 36 percent of boys having reported experiencing such pressure. The Ungdata surveys correspondingly show that Norwegian students are reporting being exposed to the most stress and pressure in Year 10 in lower secondary school and in Year 3 in upper secondary school.[16] In other words, the experience of stress and pressure does not seem to be associated with the school work itself but with the consequences this has outside school.

One reason for the growing distress that many students are experiencing, girls in particular, is that in the past, young people were forced to navigate a disciplining for the future in which the school becomes the most important arena to be mastered and that provides the key to later higher education, work and career.[17] While working life previously offered more opportunities and chances, even for those who were not quite as focused or school-smart. Rather than encouraging young people to become better at managing responsibility for their own lives, one might therefore try to reduce the pressure in the first place and, for example, show greater patience with young people's struggles in finding their place in life. One question that arises is about whether the introduction of life skills in school must also be understood against the background of increasing impatience with the struggles of young people in finding their way. Sociologist Kristoffer Chelsom Vogt has previously shown how the problem of boys dropping out of high school (*so-called drop-outs*) appears to be quite different if you operate with a more spacious window of time, which shows that many nevertheless do quite well after all, once they have become young adults.[18] Unfortunately, on the other hand, the education system in Norway today seems to be characterised by a limited spaciousness according to Vogt: "Kindergartens, daycare facilities and schools have become overloaded with ambitions. In addition, an increasing focus on the future return on investment in children and young people breeds new forms of impatience".[19] The ambitions on behalf of the young or the profitability argument are also never far away in the zeal for life skills in school.

Life is to be endured, after all

Although some aspects of life are probably more demanding today than before, there is also something about the actual problem descriptions of young people's lives that clearly should be challenged. The conceptual stress and pressure is incorporated as the actual key to understanding the life challenges of young people in Norway today, with several pages in the Ungdata report. It is considered such a major problem that a separate interdisciplinary subject is introduced to help students deal with it. But how well do we really understand these phenomena? If there is a significant ambiguity around what life mastery should be, can it be related to the fact that the core categories of stress and pressure are also rather unclear? You will immediately associate stress and pressure with the present, but there is much to suggest that they have been with us for quite some time already. The first encounter with the peculiar binary phrase in the National Library archives dates back to 1958. In the Dagbladet column "Powder and Pills", Elisabet Christensen warns that the technological advances of the time do not seem to give a corresponding boost in feelings of happiness:

> We have an Easter holiday in the mountains and vitamins in glass jars, shiny floors and all kinds of aids in our sterile laboratory kitchens. And we have stress. We can hardly get around the fact that progress and standards and increasing leisure time have paved the way for stress, pressure on the soul or whatever we may prefer to call this, our new situation.[20]

Christensen's concern is that the pursuit of constant improvement will soon exceed man's endurance and paradoxically inflict greater soulful damage on man than good along the way. During this period, stress and pressure are used almost as hustle and bustle but adapted to a new era, where you are about to leave the hustle and bustle of daily life due to new technological solutions and better economy for more and more people. As Donald Fagen sings in the opening of *The Nightfly* on the faith of the future from this era: "What a beautiful world this will be/What a wonderful time to be free".[21] But even if you got a laboratory kitchen with all the different aids, leisure time in the consumer society was not strictly free but instead another arena to be exploited to the fullest. Stress and pressure therefore became a concern, not least on behalf of women. In 1963, Consultant physician Eivind Eik of VG provides insight into how the Breast Milk Centre experiences declining deliveries from the beleaguered half of Oslo. The reason is uncertain but Eik wonders if it is related to changing times: "There's also a possibility that the stress and pressures of time have an adverse effect on milk production but it can't be proven".[22] The unease for the young people and the notion that everyday school life puts stress and pressure on students already existed at the time. The somewhat confused generation of parents appears both demanding and worried at the same time: I think you talk so much about stress and pressure and things like that but the grades pressure certainly originates from yourself. Why can't you brag a little and be nice when on random occasions we get some good grades? is pondered in the "Young People Who Always Ask" column that appeared in Nationen in 1963.[23] The conceptual pair were apparently so incorporated already at the time that there were also critical voices who were fed up with it, as here in the anonymous ironic commentary "Stress and Pressure" from the Lofoten Post from 1968:

> Now you've been arguing about stress for years. Everyone is stressed, it is an indisputable fact. Although we are now twice as stressed and pressured into half of what we once were: a young man with both steel in his chest and partial steel both here and there. As the responsible person and the good citizen that we strive to be at all times, we went in some time ago to abolish stress and pressure.[24]

However, the attempt to abolish stress and pressure proves futile as the writer ends up being sued by Apotekforeningen, the Norwegian Psychiatric Association and the manufacturers of nerve tablets, which leads to the following laconic conclusion: "A significant part of our society lives on stress and pressure".[25]

Stressed by stress

Stress can be denoted as:

> a vaguely defined concept that encompasses a mental or physiological condition characterised by – or external events or situations that lead to – a subjective experience of being under pressure to such an extent that it is perceived as unpleasant and burdensome.[26]

To a great extent, we treat stress as an objective mental or physiological condition in children and adolescents, whereas in reality we should discuss the use of stress as a term for understanding and helping with the challenges faced by young people today. The doctrine of stress as a bodily condition is compulsory in most health education programmes. During our studies of psychology, we got a thorough introduction to the physiology of stress, the fight or flight response, positive and negative stress and the prolonged, health-damaging stress of the memorable physician, Holger Ursin who held as an obsession that stress is not dangerous but actually necessary to be alive at all. The alternative – no physiological activation – is a lot worse. Despite having researched it himself, Ursin was concerned that stress was a term that was easy to mis-use. In the Aftenposten report "Stress in Fashion" from 1997, he expresses his frustration that it has become almost high status to be stressed: "I don't understand what people mean when they say they are stressed".[27] Instead, he calls for using the term "time pressure" for the challenges of being in a hurry. While today these terms have long since been incorporated into an insepara-ble duo. Ursin's fight against the inflation of stress proved to be in vain. And perhaps this is because stress today is not only abused, as he argued, but that the concept is changing and thus includes a lot more phenomena than before.

Social worker Dana Becker, in her book *One Nation Under Stress: The Trouble with Stress as an Idea,* gives a historical analysis of stress as a term in which she claims this.[28] According to Becker, stress was originally a term for a demanding situation that had to be endured. One image that was often used was a sailing ship being tossed around by the stress of bad weather. Today that sounds strange. The 1949 edition of the Merriam-Webster academic dictionary defined stress as: "The effect of external forces; especially towards overload", without reference to people. This is also reminiscent of what Ulrich Beck says about individualisation. Although today we can still understand stress as a force outside the person, emphasis is increasingly being placed on it as an internal state. The stress has become a natural part of the self, while in the past it was a force that pushed in from the outside. Thus, stress has also changed from being a temporary ordeal that our ancestors had to put up with to some-thing constant that we carry with us, which we must constantly overcome: The enemy within us. This also shortens the path to accountability by various stressed groups in society – what Becker calls stressism. And as Becker points out, this has a clear ideological gain: "The concept of stress draws the outside in – in a way that makes us end up believing that we have to change ourselves in order to adapt to the social conditions, rather than change the conditions".[29] Becker also sees the tremendous growth in what is understood to be stress in the 20th and 21st centuries in terms of phenomena such as poverty and gender equality, as an expression of the dominance of liberal individualism, where it is the individual who must change and not the external social conditions under which the individual lives. However, Becker emphasises that the stress that different groups feel is considered real but that the concept of stress provides guidelines for certain ways of being human and certain ways in which society can and should act in terms of stress, which could have been different. Other concepts could have led our pattern of reaction in other directions and to other patterns of action.

Stress in appropriate doses is necessary for us. However, the problem with stress is not only the hectic everyday life and school life of young people, it also lies in the fact that the stress discourse itself invites little more than individual stress management. Therefore, there is also reason to ask whether well-intentioned measures such as health and life skills in schools will ease the stress. Is it also the case that in the eagerness to prevent students from feeling stress and pressure, you both introduce and legitimise it? My daughter Ingebjørg started in Year 1 last fall. And at her school, all students in Year 1 get an individual visit from the school public health nurse. She told me that she was looking forward to this because she had seen that others in the class who had been to the health nurse had been given a stress ball. She then asked me: "What does stress mean?" Stress balls for all students in Year 1 – no matter how innocent they may appear – might prove to be an elastic but still not fully understood measure in which the instrument is introduced before the problem even exists.

The pressure paradox

In his book *The Ethics of Authenticity*, philosopher Charles Taylor emphasises individualism as the primary gain of modern civilisation, as most people now have a right to choose for themselves and are no longer victims of dogmatic religious or political doctrines.[30] The 1950s is when pressure first appears and is often associated with the celebration of the individual as a consumer who can now create an identity and a life via free choices on the market of goods, services and experiences. Therefore, it is essentially illogical to start talking about stress in the age of individualism, where freedom and rights represent the core values. From an etymological perspective, stress means to be under strong influence and is synonymous with words such as pressure, coercion, tyranny, freedom and duty. Concepts that one would expect to flourish primarily in totalitarian regimes or religious sects. How is this connected?

One explanation may be that all the attention around stress – eventually and gradually in ever new forms[31] – is the real child of individualism, where as a natural consequence of the newfound right of self-determination, we reacted increasingly to demands directed at us from external bodies. The duet by Queen and David Bowie, "Under Pressure (Ding Ding Ding Diddle Ing Ding)" is introduced by the lines: "Pressure pushing down on me/Pressing down on you, no man ask for",[32] therefore lies not the key to understanding pressure only as an expression of 1980s hard Thatcherism but probably just as much in the expectation of life of not having something imposed on you that you didn't choose, while in the hard days there was hardly any expectation of choosing or deciding everything yourself. The daily struggle left no further room for it. Stress is therefore a modern invention and a necessary consequence of freedom. And therefore, it is far from given that you can ever get rid of stress. It is more tempting to think that it will relentlessly be something that follows the expectation of always being able to decide what to do for yourself. Understood in this way, it also seems logical that it is the school that the young people themselves identify as being the greatest source of stress as opposed to social media for example.[33] In school, they are subject to requirements that no one has asked for. The question is whether today's students can reasonably expect to escape achievement pressures altogether, which they themselves define as "when you perform to the extent that you no longer do it for yourself but to satisfy the requirements of others".[34] Despite his inherent defence of individualism, Charles Taylor warns against a development in which we no longer accept that anyone but ourselves makes demands on us: "We may still need to understand ourselves as part of a larger context that can place requirements on us".[35] And this is both for our own sake that we do not develop an identity characterised by trivial narcissism and for the sake of the outside world. Taylor argues that the requirement to take care of nature is precisely such an example. However, there does not seem to be a lack of climate engagement among young people today. Fortunately, some requirements are still acceptable.

Who will profit from life mastery?

So why are we so concerned with stress and pressure? As mentioned, Norwegian politicians respond on the basis of widespread concern about generational achievement, where stress, pressure and mental health problems are characteristics. In my previous book *Deconstructing Scandinavia's "Achievement Generation": A Youth Mental Health Crisis?* one of the main messages was that this generational description and contemporary diagnosis has only partly to do with the challenges facing the young people in Norway today.[36] There is a lot to suggest that generational achievement is a notion rooted in the upper middle class, where it is taken for granted that all Norwegian youth are struggling with stress and pressure to get the best possible grade in school, in order to realise themselves and their full potential. But not all young Norwegian people struggle with exaggerated ambitions and requirements for perfection. Those who suffer the most are more likely to struggle with dysfunctional family relationships, poor advice, bullying, intoxication, genetic diseases, abuse, neglect, exclusion and school expulsion. One explanation for the idea of generational achievement might be that we live in an individualised, classless society where mental disorders are understood as apolitical and disconnected from inequality, economics and ideology. But there is also a clear correlation between the family finances and the proportion of mental health problems that young people report. Fifty-five percent of those who feel that "The family has poor affordability all the time" report four to six health problems, while only twelve percent in the group who state that the family has "Good affordability all the time", state the corresponding extent of problems.[37] The perception of the successful youth who are also struggling – generational achievement – probably became popular in the media in the mid-2010s because it is a more welcome media template. Being successful but mentally ill is simply more interesting and click-friendly than being disabled and mentally ill. Although the latter provides a more truthful picture of which young people are struggling the most. And speaking of life mastery, the question about whether measures that place relatively high requirements on the self-effort of the students actually capture the less articulated part of the young people who are not particularly ambitious on their own behalf, are not as resourceful or involved in their schoolwork and who may not even be physically or mentally present in teaching. Thus, it is an obvious danger that a measure such as health and life skills in schools reproduces the already well-known dilemma from the adult world, where there are always the same resourceful, engaged and "good" parents who show up at lectures for parents and young people for the purposes of the Parents' Working Committee (FAU), sign up for municipal courses in parental guidance and keep up to date with what the experts think at all times about good and poor upbringings, such as the popular Aftenposten podcast, *Parenting Code*, whereas the group that might really need it never gets it. The code seems harder to crack. Furthermore, the Norwegian Institute of Public Health population studies indicate that around seven percent of school-age children have symptoms consistent with a mental illness.[38] Here, it is primarily measures other than life mastery that are needed. These young people will usually have a need for help beyond what the school can reasonably offer and will probably need treatment in mental health care for children and adolescents (BUP).

Risk society

The notion of youth at risk can also be understood on the basis of how risk has generally become more prominent in late modernity. With the contemporary diagnosis of the risk society, Ulrich Beck points out how earlier disasters such as famine, earthquakes or plague are today overshadowed by new risks that are not originally naturally related but are themselves an inevitable result of progress and scientific and social changes, whether nuclear accidents, climate change or genetically modified organisms.[39] And while in ancient times disasters were primarily local, the dangers of our time are global. The coronavirus pandemic in 2020 is a sadly relevant example of how the threats today are spreading a lot faster and further than before. Climate change, such as the icecap melting at the poles increases the potential to spread COVID-19 and viruses of this type, as different animals and humans are brought closer together.[40] Understood in this way, there is little reason to doubt that young people today are confronted with increased pressure and new requirements. And to deal with the inherent risks of world development in the 21st century, it is natural to imagine that to a greater extent than before, young people must be prepared to face more crises. The Ludvigsen Committee emphasises this in the following:

> Each individual must make mindful and conscious decisions in many areas, including decisions related to their own health, social relations, sustainable consumption and their own economy. When in many areas society is characterised by individualisation, it can give great freedom to individual choice but it can also increase the requirements on the individual.[41]

But although the Committee also refers to Beck's risk society in a footnote, the solution it presents – life mastery and more self-regulation – is hardly in keeping with the same spirit as Beck. As mentioned, he was critical of the tendency for the individual to be increasingly asked to find biographical solutions to systemic crises. But this trend only seems to be continuing. A recent study of the EU cross-sector youth strategy since 2000 targeted at young people at risk finds a link between economic downturns such as the financial crisis and policy initiatives that were implemented to mitigate the consequences, where attempts are made to develop the individual competitiveness and flexibility of young people.[42] The researchers therefore warn against the normalisation of a neoliberal political rationality in which politics is built around risk in young people – which is categorically always seen as at risk – while understanding the larger systemic causes is absent:

> We see a risk reduced to a view in which the individual has the problem and where it is the individual who lacks a predetermined sets of skills and knowledge. Instead of formulating how to curb systemic and structural unemployment, the guidelines are aimed at solving young people's unemployment individually, so that they themselves can ultimately develop a commitment to building their individual skills resources.[43]

The warning is also apt for understanding young people's lives in Norway. The answer to youth at risk is often resilience or robustness. By focusing more on mental health in school, the hope is "to give young people relevant contributions to a more robust mental health".[44] However, social worker Reidun Follesø has asked whether it is primarily youth at risk or the risk associated with our concepts of youth that is the biggest problem.[45] Follesø refers to examples from international youth research, where in recent years several authors have pointed to how we not only use the language but how the language uses us and makes us understand the problems of young people in ways that in turn give rise to problematic solutions. Kitty te Riele argued that the political solutions to youth at risk tend to neglect collective and structural conditions in schools and society and instead present the problems as challenges for the young.[46] Karen Foster and Dale Spence argued that risk and resilience understanding of young people's lives limit their opportunities within this discursive framework.[47] The desire for "resilient kids" is understandable but at the same time, tells of a time when the utopian ideals of another society have disappeared.

Accountability

Both young people and adults have also expressed concern that life skills in school is just another thing that the already quite responsible young people have to master and take responsibility for. The Change Factory, which spoke to around 5,000 students during the development of the life mastery programme *The LIFE Hour*, states that despite the desire for life mastery, many of the students with whom they spoke say that: "Life mastery must not become another thing that we have to master".[48] Adult actors have also expressed similar reservations, including Mina Gerhardsen, Secretary General of the National Association for Public Health: "For example, when the school is to strengthen life skills and health, this must not be something that students should primarily learn as practical tips and advice, then [sic] it becomes something they have to take individual responsibility for".[49] Even the Ludvigsen Committee, which is one of the main architects of health and life skills in schools, sees this pitfall based on experiences from the school reforms of the 1990s.

It seems appropriate here to draw in the well-known duck test, which is often invoked in the face of abstruse arguments that something is not what it looks like: "If something looks like a duck, swims like a duck and quacks like a duck, then it is probably a duck". In the influential transactional stress model of psychologists Richard Lazarus and Susan Folkman, stress first arises from a perceived discrepancy between the requirements of a situation and the resources the individual has to deal with them. In the report *Stress and Coping*, Oddrun Samdal, Bente Wold Anette Harris and Torbjørn Torsheim, researchers from the HEMIL Centre, comment on the model:

> An important premise of this understanding is that the individual's experience can be changed by adjusting both the experience of their own resources for example, in the form of providing social support and by adjusting the requirements and expectations of the immediate environment (at home and in school/work space) so that they are in line with the ability of the individual to fulfil them. Good financial support schemes in the event of unemployment are examples of more overarching national decisions that also have an impact on the individual perception of stress in uncertain economic times, but which can be more time-consuming to change as they require political decisions.[50]

In theory, the imbalance between external requirements and individual resources can just as easily be solved by adjusting expectations from the environment. Transferring students in school will mean changing the requirements that make many people experience a high degree of stress and pressure. As mentioned, young people report being subject to the most stress and pressure in Year 10 in lower secondary school and in Year 3 in upper secondary school.[51] One explanation may be that during these graduation years, many students are stressed by the pressure to get good enough grades that will ensure them the freedom of choice to enter upper secondary school or the higher education they want. The Government now wants to introduce free school choice as a compulsory admission scheme for upper secondary schools in all counties in Norway, while the Education Association has opposed the proposal because in reality it means that only the brightest will be able to choose schools freely.[52] Free school choice is a scheme that is very political and could be changed. Grade-based admission could be as well.

But when designing life mastery as a school subject, the second strategy has been chosen: To try to equip students with coping strategies to be better able to cope with the stress and pressure. Naturally, this has the obvious advantage of not having to meet the requirements and make resource-intensive changes to the system. And if the intervention is successful, it means that the resources of the individual student to manage stress both in school and later in life are strengthened. What is right will depend on the outcome, which also involves a dilemma regarding how much responsibility it is reasonable to expect young people to take for their own situation, whether concern is primarily directed at helping those with resources or those lacking resources and ultimately, what kind of disease and human vision you have and which political ideology you advocate. If we consult the "bible" of stress research – Lazarus and Folkman's red brick of a book from 1984, *Stress, Appraisal, and Coping* – they acknowledge that whether you seek to change the environment or the individual is undoubtedly a political question: "These two perspectives, the people who shape and the human who is being shaped, have striking political implications".[53] And by extension, they leave no doubt about which political ideology underlies understanding negative outcomes solely as a result of coping errors:

> The notion that lack of integration and disease is due to a lack of coping is consistent with conservative political ideology, which focuses on the shortcomings of the person rather than the environment, which is encapsulated in the line from Shakespeare in *Julius Caesar*: "The fault, dear Brutus, is not in the stars but in ourselves".[54]

They choose to be pragmatic themselves: They write that as it is neither possible to create a perfect social order nor to make an individual the perfect coping machine, the choice must be made between the solution that seems most suitable for the problem that you have front of you. However, the question is whether since the 1980s this issue of value has shifted so much that today, in the eagerness to produce perfect coping machines, there is no longer any reflection on the fact that the attempt to strengthen the individual's coping resources is also the result of a wanted policy that could have been different. The NOVA researcher Eriksen previously mentioned found in the survey of the experience of stress and pressure among students in schools in Oslo, that the possibility of protesting against or removing the stress on the body that they experience did not even appear as an opportunity for the students, which may indicate precisely such a shift.[55] A first step towards a better understanding of the problems of young people and thus of society, is therefore to become aware that things could have been different.

Is life mastery apolitical?

All political parties support life mastery in school. Thus, it is not obvious that it comes with any political denomination even though it was adopted under the blue-blue government. The appointment of the Ludvigsen Committee was undertaken by the red-green government, while the Christian Democratic Party was the party that first took the initiative to the Storting. On the other hand, the equation is balanced if we assume that all political parties have fallen to their knees for a new way of conducting politics in a less value-oriented and all the more technocratic way. Moreover, the primary goal of life mastery is for students to become experts on themselves. Sociologist Dag Leonardsen has described how in the 1980s Norwegian politicians began to flag their own powerlessness and emphasise the responsibility of the individual for their situation.[56] He writes that, "The development also undermined the collective political responsibility in favour of individual responsibility within social democracy in line with the increased influence of neoliberalism". One example is the New Year's address from 1992 by then Prime Minister Gro Harlem Brundtland, best known for the famous but in retrospect somewhat misunderstood slogan, "It is typically Norwegian to be good", in which Brundtland reformulates the solidarity welfare society and puts it into the framework for the new individualised era that lies ahead of us. For example, via twists similar to the Orwellian Newspeak: "New opportunities for the individual | help to self-help | Solidarity means that we require everyone | To take responsibility for our fellow human beings does not mean that we should take responsibility from them".[57]

If introducing a measure such as life skills in school because as the Ludvigsen Committee admits, increased individualisation requires greater skills in "taking responsibility for your own life",[58] it seems appropriate to ask whether this is an exact example of what Leonardsen calls the abdication of politics. This is by no means unique to Norway but typical of the emergence of newer advanced liberal ways of governing as seen in the USA, Australia, New Zealand, the UK and Scandinavia, which involves a profound change in the traditional way of thinking and practicing politics. Traditional welfare states seek to govern via society, while now a life policy is sought that is as free as possible from the state, where you govern in line with the measurable choices of the individuals. According to sociologist Nikolas Rose, a discipline such as psychology thus acquires a distinctive status as a governing expertise as it can mobilise the individual and oversee how the individual lives, without it being perceived as abuse of power or inconsistent interference on the part of the authorities.[59] Psychology can offer a variety of practices that help people to govern themselves. Despite a somewhat broad content, life mastery can be understood as such self-technology. Although Rose points out that the tendency to pursue politics as a more individual form of governance in the first place applies to both the left and the right, it seems that the popularity of psychology in Norway is greatest amongst the latter. In any case, it is a fact that in recent years, mental health has often been promoted by the Conservative Party and its long-reigning Minister of Health and Care Services, Bent Høie.

Before the municipal and county council elections in 2015, editor-in-chief of the *Journal of the Norwegian Psychological Association*, Bjørnar Olsen wrote about this hegemony: "The Conservatives still seem to have a tight monopoly on mental health in the political debate – just as they did before the 2013 general election".[60] Olsen admits that this may simply be due to the respect the other parties have for Høie but wonders if there is an elective affinity between psychology and right-wing solutions: "Or perhaps the right-wing enthusiasm is due to the fact that in psychology they see a subject that offers solutions to the health challenges of society that align with their liberalist views of humanity".[61] In this case, it will mean that the individual must work on themselves rather than the authorities working to change the environment and disease-creating structures. The relevant backdrop for Olsen's analysis at the time was the Solberg government's proposal to legislate for all municipalities to have a psychologist by 2020, for which the Norwegian Psychological Association had been fighting for political support for years. And where the ranks of Labour Party health ministers had been relatively lukewarm, they now had a long-awaited ally in the Conservative Party. But Olsen asks: At what cost? He notes how the municipal psychologist initiative throughout Norway makes it easier for more psychologists to be heard in the sense of more therapists but not as social psychologists who conduct municipal planning and preventive health work. Thus, this also becomes a Faustic pact for psychology, as the alliance not only expands certain parts of the subject but also narrows other parts of it: "Psychological traditions that violate individualism receive no political help and thus do not become part of the measures and solutions at the societal level. In this way, politics also narrows psychology as both a subject and as a practice".[62] However, Olsen is not a fatalist on behalf of psychology and demands that the opposition come to the fore via a collectivist, preventive approach to how good mental health is not primarily created in the health service but in families, kindergartens, daycare facilities, schools and working life. Naturally, it can be argued that life skills in school is precisely such a measure, but does it strictly address the need for a preventive social policy that Olsen is calling for here, or must it be characterised as pseudo-prevention?

History of the fall of prevention

If we look to the municipalities, there is currently much talk about prevention but in a distinct manner. "Want to prevent depression among young people" was a feature of the NRK *District News for Østfold* just before it had to give way to Viken. The newsreader introduced the report as follows: "According to figures from Ungdata, 20% of young people in Råde and Moss are plagued by symptoms of depression. The average in Østfold is 16%. Measures have been taken in Råde to help people early".[63] A brief interview with Conservative Mayor René Rafshol followed, and he explained what the municipality does:

> First of all, of course we have moved psychiatry to the field of upbringing because we see there is a connection. It is important to collaborate in an interdisciplinary manner as quickly as possible. We have established a youth team here at lower secondary school level back here, with a psychiatric nurse. We want to continue with this into primary school and also in kindergartens and daycare facilities. We are seeing that mental health problems are starting earlier and earlier. To do things early, we also need to get in early with an intervention.[64]

In the interview, salutations such as interdisciplinary and early intervention pop up, and Rafshol emphasises the connection between growing up and psychiatry. But it doesn't appear to be that the politicians in Råde envision very significant changes in the conditions of the upbringing of children in the municipality. Instead, the early intervention strategy will equip a team of experts with a psychiatric nurse who will go into lower secondary school and preferably into primary school, kindergarten and daycare facilities. This news story on how local efforts are being made to "prevent" depression in Norway illustrates how the idea of prevention is simply changing from politics to psychology. And from creating the least possible economic differences and an integrative local environment to initiating efforts as early as possible, where prevention is individualised, "clinified" and "technified".

This development is not unique to Råde municipality but seems to have become the norm around the country and given much impetus along its way by professionals.

> In Bærum municipality, they have long since realised the importance of preventive efforts for mental health in children and young people. They are teaching psychological first aid in primary and secondary school. Now the kindergartens and daycare facilities are next.[65]

This is the introduction to a "happy case" from the Norwegian Association for Cognitive Therapy concerning the Bærum municipality's embracing of psychologist specialist Sofrid Raknes' *Psychological First Aid* kits. The popular self-help kits with the green and red thought figures have been developed on the basis of internationally recognised treatment programmes such as *Mestringskatten* and *FRIENDS for Life*. Thus, it is an example of how treatment tools that are based on cognitive behavioural therapy are granted broad access and are no longer reserved just for the therapy room. Now they are going into the everyday life of every child, preferably as early as possible. In

Bærum municipality, there is broad political agreement to introduce teaching in *Psychological First Aid* in Years 2, 5 and 8. The starting point for the desire to introduce the self-help steps for all students in both primary and secondary schools was the 2014 Ungdata survey, which is claimed to have revealed that many young people felt subject to stress and pressure. In Ringsaker municipality, the decision has already been made to start using *Psychological First Aid* from kindergarten age: "All children in Ringsaker municipality will learn about feelings, thoughts and be able to develop good skills in self-care".[66] There is an ongoing change in the thinking about prevention, which increasingly seems to be moving away from economic equalisation and social inclusion. Instead, it is possible for all children and adolescents to undertake some form of cognitive self-care from an early age, in order to develop "a psychological immune system".[67] On one hand, the early intervention rhetoric aims to ensure that "everyone is included" and that everyone is given the same starting point through the introduction of programmes into kindergartens, daycare facilities and schools, but on the other hand, it reflects only to a small extent that the differences in the learning starting points for children involve different conditions in terms of upbringing.

Which edition of psychology represents life mastery?

As much as life mastery reveals a leading political doctrine, it is also about a prescriptive psychological approach. For many decades, the psychoanalysis of Sigmund Freud (1856–1939) was the dominant model for the talking therapy, while today it is common to count cognitive behavioural therapy (CBT) as the new gold standard of psychotherapy.[68] For a time, even the dominance of CBT was so strong that the health authorities in countries such as Sweden and the United Kingdom passed legislation making psychotherapeutic treatment and education cognitively oriented.[69] Although the alignment is not quite as obvious today and some even believe that psychoanalysis is about to have its renaissance,[70] there are several obvious reasons for considering life skills in school as an extension of the prevalence of cognitive psychotherapy. Some of the most influential psychoeducational programmes that have already been in use in school for Norway for several years, such as *Mestringskatten*, *Zippy's Friends* and *Psychological First Aid* are explicitly based on the fundamental principles of CBT. This is probably due to the fact that there is a clearer link between cognitive therapy and the self-help philosophy than in the other psychotherapy specialisations. In the primer in cognitive therapy, *The Inner Dialogue*, psychologists Torkil Berge and Arne Repål elaborate on the connection: "[C]ognitive therapy is primarily help to self-help, where the patient learns to become his/her own therapist".[71] Central to this is the vision that the client will eventually gain expert skills in their own thought processes and regulate themselves to the greatest extent possible. This idea is also found again in the Ludvigsen Committee NOU report on the skills that students in

The School of the Future will need, highlighting psychological variables such as metacognition and self-regulation, which deal precisely with gaining skills in their own thought and learning processes and their own behavioural patterns. It is probably also not coincidental that APA President George Miller, who launched the vision of the psychological revolution in which citizens of the future society should serve as their own psychologists, was one of the scientific pioneers of the cognitive revolution of the 1950s. But almost as long-lasting as the importance of cognitive psychotherapy is the criticism of its possible ideological slant(s). In 1990, psychologist Isaac Prilleltensky wrote about the social and political implications of cognitive psychology, noting how cognitive forms of therapy had made a name for themselves not only in the therapy rooms but also in the school system of the USA during the previous decade. According to Prilleltensky, the reason for its popularity here was not difficult to understand:

> Just as governing bodies prefer a "thought fix" over an "environment fix", many school principals, teachers and parents prefer "thought" therapies that deal with the child, while the adults, the classroom and the social order in school remain unchanged.[72]

Prilleltensky was particularly worried that psychologists inadvertently risk *blaming the victim* when, in line with the postulates of cognitive psychotherapy, they consider the negative mind content of someone suffering depression to be a pure product of disturbed thought processes, without taking into account that thinking reflects a negative reality in which the person suffering from depression lives. This may sound obvious, but the fact is that since Prilleltensky wrote this, the medical model and the ethos of cognitive psychology have gained high degree of hegemony, so that seemingly common social psychological postulates such as: "People do not have mental illnesses; people live or have lived in environments that do not support healthy behaviours" today come out under titles such as *How to Rethink Mental Illness*.[73]

Lack of emotional intelligence

What is an emotion? Where do emotions come from? What do our emotions tell us? If these questions sound familiar, it is probably because you've had a half-watchful eye on contemporary culture – whether educational children's television or self-help and management literature for adult children – and for men in particular, who do *not* know their feelings. In the NRK series *Innafor* on current contemporary themes, the episode "The Man" was all about why men are so poor at talking about emotions compared to women. Here, being able to share emotions is elevated to being the (sole) thing that matters: "And when we share emotions, we have value for one another other".[74] Despite the opposition NRK investigative reporter Vilde Bratland Eriksen encounters

from evolutionary psychologist Leif Edward Ottesen Kennair when it came to
the notion that men have an innate handicap and that it is exclusively positive
to put into words everything you feel, the episode ironically ends with the
recognition: "No, I still feel that my theory is correct".[75]

This stream of consciousness is often referred to as the *emotional revolution*. The name is intended as a corrective to the cognitive revolution in
psychology with its starting point being that the importance of emotions has
been given too little space in the understanding of man and in social design.[76]
The movement has also made a name for itself in the requirements for life
mastery, where students are also expected to learn to express, share and manage their own and others' emotions. As was recently pointed out in an Aftenposten column signed by professionals from the field of mental health, who
accused the government of not following up on mental health and life skills
in the proposed new school curriculum: "Emotions have important functions
in life mastery. No emotion, no life mastery. How we feel is governed by and
governs how we perceive and think".[77]

Historically, supporters of the emotional revolution are correct when they
say that emotion has been neglected and regarded as volatile, unreliable and
irrational. They are also right that it is a matter of getting to know their emotions. The alternative is that as adults, we react as immature children in any
situation where we may feel ignored or violated. And this thought is far from
new. Aristotle (384–322 B.C.) had already stated that in order to become a
capable citizen, man must raise his feelings.[78] But it's still as if this is no
longer enough. The requirement has now been made stricter to include sharing
and talking about their feelings and showing sufficient psychological openness. And if the majority of the population does not immediately acknowledge
that they share their feelings with others, it is perceived as a strong signal
that mental health must be included at kindergartens, daycare facilities and in
school. The argument is often further cemented with a socioeconomic calcula-
tion that shows that it will save Norway so many millions a year,[79] as if deep
down, there is really not enough confidence that an appeal to the emotions is
enough to win.

This strong superstitious belief in the importance of emotions is evident
in the previously cited *The Book That is Missing*, which wants to get mental health and life skills on the school timetable. The remark, "But the ABC
of thought, emotions and actions is not in the schoolbag" suggests that so
far, Norwegian students have to be considered as psychologically illiterate
after finishing school,[80] whereas in contrast to having learned the alphabet
and basic reading and writing skills, they completely lack the knowledge that
gives them "maps and compasses for the mental terrain".[81] In launching the
appeal, the President of the Norwegian Psychological Association also introduces a related analogy: "We need a gym class for thoughts and feelings!"[82]
Here, the message is repeated that Norwegian students must learn "how
to maintain good mental health – just as much as the students learn about

anatomy, physical education and nutrition".[83] But the analogies are lame. It is quite obvious to everyone that you have to know letters to be able to read and write. It is not as obvious that you have to know the composition of your body in order to use it. Nor that Norwegian students strictly need some gym lessons in order to be able to use their bodies. It does what we want it to do without our having any knowledge of its anatomical composition and can be stretched gymnastically. Crawling, walking, running and jumping come naturally in the first years of life for the vast majority of children. If you want to become a physiotherapist or chiropractor or play top-level sports, it may of course be necessary to have specialised bodily skills, but for the vast majority, the body works completely by itself in its everyday tasks, without any significant knowledge of its structure or plasticity. And so it is with emotions for the vast majority of people. They help us function and interact with other people in everyday life, without necessarily being able to figure out what an emotion is or where it comes from. However, on the other hand, the initiators behind *The Book That is Missing* ask the school to teach students about the psyche in order for them to then be able to use this lexical mental doctrine to communicate with the outside world via rehearsed emotional objects such as green and red thoughts.

The analogy also seems to have been picked up by our elected representatives. When Iselin Nybø of the Liberal Party introduced life skills in the schools for consideration in the Storting, she stated how physical expression has already been incorporated in the school, adding: "But we are not as good at teaching how we can train and take care of our psyche".[84] It is understandable that we want the psyche and its disorders to receive the same recognition as the body and its diseases, but the juxtaposition risks narrowing the psyche to a manipulatable size that one is constantly responsible for activating and that is lifted out of its sociocultural context and relational context of meaning. At the same time, as children and young people are presented with some easy-to-understand mental gymnastic categories, they must sort them. While the model drawings of children and adolescents in the psychological first aid kits are striding around in contextless realities, they are surrounded only by their dichotomous train of thought.[85] Psychology is then sold back to the population in inviting, democratic terms: "Everyone has a mental health".[86]

Another psychology is possible

However, it is possible to envision mental health and life mastery in school done in a different way than the cognitively modelled one. Psychologists Ida Brandtzæg, Stig Torsteinson and Guro Øiestad, authors of the book *See the Student From Within*, have expressed enthusiasm that the Norwegian Psychological Association has finally succeeded in getting life mastery on the school timetable. In the same breath, they have also expressed concern for the chosen design of mental health and life skills in school, as it primarily targets the students themselves rather than their teachers:

> At the same time, it is remarkable how much confidence there is that teaching about mental health should help the students, rather than strengthening the relationship between teacher and student. It is good that in the future the students will gain knowledge about mental health but we believe it is clearly more important that teachers gain knowledge and awareness of the importance of the relationship, so that they are helped to reflect in a systematic way on the encounter with the students and that this is not left to the discretion of the teacher.[87]

In this respect, one can envision a more relational psychology as a substitute for individual-oriented cognitive psychology's belief in teaching children and young people to monitor and regulate their own thought and learning processes. Nevertheless, it is reasonable to assume that skilled teachers already possess the skills to see the individual and establish good, trusting relationships with all students, even though this is not necessarily stated. Nonetheless, an increased systematic focus on relational competence among teachers will mean that it is not randomness and the personal style of the individual teacher that determines whether this is fulfilled, a conclusion that has also been emphasised by special needs teacher Ingrid Lund.[88] Despite the fact that the general part of the curriculum has the development of relational competence as a goal, she sees a tendency that in the school governance documentation, this must constantly give way to requirements for competence within the core subjects. The Norwegian Directorate of Health database of programmes for public health work in the municipalities also shows that the majority of the relevant measures concerning life mastery in schools focus on training the students, not the teachers.[89]

In a more social psychology approach, it could also be envisaged that the measures were put in place not only among teachers and in teacher education but amongst school management and responsible politicians tasked with preventive work at the system level. These include strengthening the psychological-pedagogical service (PPT) into the school management team to exercising an independent critical-constructive function rather than merely conducting investigation and individual guidance – which has been advocated by pedagogue Peder Haug,[90] to measures such as ensuring that schools have fewer students per teacher and free school meals, to equalising social inequality in the municipalities via housing for vulnerable groups and free core time in kindergartens and daycare facilities. It is thus possible to welcome mental health into school but problematise the way in which it is currently being done. Not least because the actual loss of life mastery places so much responsibility on young shoulders.

It doesn't have to be so bad

I initially noted that the authorities have designed the life mastery project very broadly, and one argument may of course also be that it is simply too early to say what form the spacious subject of health and life skills in schools will have, as well as how dutifully different schools and teachers will be in following up on the subject. It does not necessarily have to be another subject for the students to master and another reason why they should take responsibility for the stress and pressures in everyday school life and in life outside. At best, it could become an interdisciplinary subject that develops what the school already does: Arouse student interest in something greater outside themselves and where mastery is experienced indirectly as a result of such engagement through which each student realises his/her interests and abilities, whether physical, artisanal, artistic or contemplative. In reality, this has always been the ambition of the schools even before the renewal of the Knowledge Promotion Reform. Secondary education teacher Jørg Arne Jørgensen has described his most important mission as a teacher:

> As a secondary school teacher, I see it as my most important task to get students out of the horrors that are so typical of their age, where their own feelings become what the world revolves around. If I can ignite a spark, arouse interest in something outside the self – literature, politics, the world, anything – I've done my job.[91]

However, Jørgensen is concerned about how interdisciplinary subjects such as health and life skills will be reconciled with this and asks whether implementation in a time-typical way does not imply the opposite: "I perceive a society that does the opposite – setting out to focus on its own achievements – and feeling very good about it".[92] Presumably, supporters of health and life skills in schools will object that getting students away from pondering and getting them to be more engaged in the outside world is the whole purpose of life mastery. However, it is as if students, teachers, psychologists, educators and politicians have been persuaded that to make this happen at all – that as many students as possible find their niche and place in working life and life overall – consideration must be given to generating a psychological immune system or mental resilience and that from now on, it will be the school's job to ensure it. This hierarchical view of knowledge coincides with a larger contemporary anti-humanist tendency to choose simple individual solutions to complex societal challenges but veiled in inviting rhetoric.

But of course, children and young people want it

About 100,000 children have signed the petition calling for mental health and life mastery to be introduced in schools. Perhaps young people don't know what is in their own best interests? No, and neither do adults. Philosopher Lars Johan Mastertvedt recently challenged what we often believe about ourselves: "the rhetoric of self-determination rests on a specific, problematic empirical premise: that we know what is best for us".[93] Mastertvedt gives examples from everyday situations where we subsequently admit that we have done something stupid, to actively assisted euthanasia where research has shown that people's desire to die can change within an hour. But humans have a strong tendency to constantly relate to each other as if we always know what is in our own best interests. Mastertvedt links the belief in self-determination to the rise of individualism in the West, where, in line with the core values of liberalism, the individual can choose for herself and is thus also regarded as being responsible for all her actions. One may wonder whether the life challenges faced by young people today – popularly understood as stress and pressure – are precisely due to an expectation that children and young people will also act as free and responsible sovereigns in their own lives. And perhaps this expectation has now reached some kind of breaking point. But because we have become accustomed to liberal individualism, we cannot imagine any social medicine other than courses in stress and life mastery. And that's also what children and young people want to have on their school timetable. But in reality, the solution represents only more of the same when increased individualisation and accountability are the social drivers that have brought us into this disability. Paradoxically, even one of the nesters of self-regulation research – psychologist Roy Baumeister – admits that the large-scale individualisation experiment in the West, where everything is placed on the individual will not necessarily have a happy outcome: "It's hard to have high hopes for this experiment: maybe we're asking each individual to do too much?"[94] With health and life skills entering Norwegian schools in 2020, we are in effect asking children and young people to do *more*.

Building a "psyche"

The underlying view of humanity behind the introduction of health and life skills in school is reminiscent of the ideas in therapeutic culture, self-help literature and the coaching world, which are now also knocking on the door of Norwegian education institutions. Along with media scientist Brita Ytre-Arne, ten years ago I analysed the content of the most popular Norwegian women's magazines as part of a doctoral work on the entry of global therapeutic culture into Norway.[95] In particularly *Kvinner & Klær*, the idea of optimising oneself inspired by media mogul Oprah Winfrey amongst others, had gained repute: "No one can be anyone else but everyone can be a better version of themselves", wrote editor-in-chief Gjyri Helén Werp in the editorial "Me at My Best".[96] A few years later, while working on a book on self-help literature, I again found the idea of being the best version of oneself but now within the National Curriculum Regulations for several kindergartens in

Eastern Norway.[97] I don't really think any of the kindergartens and daycare facilities worked systematically to determine whether the toddlers had worked sufficiently well this week to become the best version of themselves. Nevertheless, the dissemination of the idea in a few years, including in Norway, testifies to a nascent change in how we think about both children and adults. The difference between "with us children shall become" and "with us children shall be allowed to become the best version of themselves" is not insignificant. The idea that young people *are* nothing in the first place but should *become* something now seems to have reached the schools in earnest. If it only meant supporting the students in their academic maturation, it would admittedly be quite uncontroversial, but there is something more on the table – not only the identity of children and young people but also their psyche, which will now be built, trained and developed through sufficient self-effort.

Occasionally, this may also be reminiscent of mental training, well known from top-level sports. As part of a carefully balanced routine training day for top athletes with a clear goal in sight, mental training can be defended. But the mental aspect has begun to live its own life rather than being considered a byproduct of performance.[98] So far, we have witnessed rising golf star Viktor Hovland – who doesn't see the point of having his own mental coach but instead thinks "that if he hits the ball well, he gains confidence";[99] his view is consistently referred to as "special"[100] and "controversial".[101] The appeal of mental training, however, is not difficult to understand. It is tempting to think that the mental sphere, not unlike a myth, always offers an explanation for why you fail or succeed. The mental resources are lying there undetected in everyone; it is only a matter of finding the right setting where you think wisely or "masterly" enough. Never mind that many people never find this resource. This is the case with mental health and life mastery as well, it has become an isolated item that young people should take advantage of, build up and exercise in rather than considering good mental health as an integrated byproduct of a safe and stable upbringing environment.

In many ways, life skills in school seems to have become a preferred apolitical way for Norwegian politicians to address the concerns of children and young people in Norway today. But this concern for young people's lives is strangely disconnected from the possible causes of the challenges. It is quite tempting in this respect to quote my philosophy teacher, Gunnar Skirbek, who, during a meeting in the Student Union Building in Bergen in the late 1990s, said: "Politics will not be interesting again until someone other than the Christian Democratic Party begins talking about values".[102] Under the initiative of the Christian Democratic Party, there was probably an idea that it is more difficult to be young today than previously due to increased secularisation and declining faith in God, especially in the younger segment of the population. It is at least a problem description rooted in values that could be challenged by other understandings of reality. But instead, it seems that during legislative processing in the Storting, the Christian Democratic Party was also forced to consider life mastery as a more life-neutral solution that everyone could get behind. And the result has been a half-thought-out and washed-out recipe in which the "big and difficult issues" related to the problems faced by young people remain unaddressed. The outcome of the renewal of the subject will thus be highly uncertain and in addition, life mastery becomes vulnerable to abuse in the absence of a clear design.

"It's not how you feel but how you cope with it" is in many cases probably a wise philosophy of life, although there is something ambiguous about the fact that stoicism has come back into fashion today,[103] but the question life mastery really raises is also whether it is a smart policy. Or is it instead an expression of the bankruptcy of politics? The original critics of the emerging therapeutic culture feared that the psychological human being of the 20th and 21st centuries would seek therapies and techniques to learn to live with the disappointment of the presumable impossibility of social, political and economic changes.[104] In short, living in a cultural climate in which life settings become everything and living conditions nothing. To adjust the diminishing expectation that another world is possible, perhaps as a start we should not expect more life mastery of our young hopefuls but first and foremost *more* of our elected adult representatives.

Thanks

Several people have helped me in the work on this book. Thanks to Anders Bakken, Hildegunn Brattvåg, Åste Dokka, Gunnar Skirbekk, Tilmann von Soest, Lars Petter Storm Torjussen and Kristoffer Chelsom Vogt for great help along the way. The Section on the Ludvigsen Committee is based on a previously published book chapter by the undersigned, who have been included the anthology *Report – Genre and Management Tools* (Pax, 2018). Thanks to the editor of the book, Kristian Bjørkdahl and Mona Ringvej of Pax publishing house for permission to use it here. I would also like to thank the editor, Sivje Felldal, of Spartacus Publishing, for her faith in this project and for good cooperation throughout the entire process. And finally, I would like to thank Grace McDonnell and Sarah Hafeez at Routledge for their helpful assistance and willingness to put out this project. This book is dedicated to my youngest son Didrik who on a daily basis disrupts any illusion I may have about coping with life, reminding me that life is primarily to be lived.

Notes

1 Craig Winston LeCroy and Elizabeth K. Anthony, "Youth at risk", *Oxford Bibliographies* (2018), www.oxfordbibliographies.com/view/document/obo-9780195389678/obo-9780195389678-0112.xml#firstMatch.
2 Ingunn B. Skre, "Resiliens [Resilience]", *Store norske leksikon* (2019), https://snl.no/resiliens.
3 The Norwegian Psychology Association et al., *Boken som mangler* [*The Book That Is Missing*], 3.

4 Jon Lid and Andreas Riis, Eds., *Studentene fra 1909* [The *Students from 1909*] (Oslo: The Mallingske Bookstore, 1959), 133.
5 Kari Halstensen, "The focus on young people's mental health can be constructive", *Aftenposten* (2020, 11.2.), www.aftenposten.no/meninger/debatt/i/naKA7B/fokuset-paa-unge-menneskers-psykiske-helse-kan-vaere-konstruktivt-kari-halstensen., dec. 25–7.
6 Knud Ejler Løgstrup, *Den etiske fordring* [*The Ethical Claimant*] (Oslo: Cappelen, 2000).
7 Ole Jacob Madsen, *Deconstructing Scandinavia's "Achievement Generation": A Youth Mental Health Crisis?* (London: Palgrave, 2021).
8 Ibid., 9.
9 Bakken, *Ungdata 2019. Nasjonale resultater* [*Ungdata 2019: National Results*].
10 Utdanningsnytt, "Rapport: 13-åringer bør få undervisning i livsmestring [Report: 13-year-olds should be taught life mastery]", *Utdanningsnytt* (2017, 24.1), www.utdanningsnytt.no/rapport-13-aringer-bor-fa-undervisning-i-livsmestring/180235.
11 Report to the Storting, Report St. 28, *Fag – Fordyådming – Forståelse. En fornyelse av Kunnskapsløftet* [*Subject-Specialisation-Understanding: A Renewal of the Knowledge Promotion Reform*].
12 Bakken, *Ungdata 2019. Nasjonale resultater* [*Ungdata 2019: National Results*].
13 Shaghayegh Yousefi, "– Det forventes mer av oss på alle arenaer [-More of us are expected in all arenas]", *Aftenposten* (2017, 10.7), sec. 26; 35.
14 Ibid., sec. 28.
15 WHO, *Growing Up Unequal: Gender and Socioeconomic Differences in Young People's Health and Well-Being* (Copenhagen: WHO, 2016).
16 Bakken, *Ungata 2019. Nasjonale resultater* [*Ungdata 2019: National Results*].
17 Kristinn Hegna, Guro Ødegård, and Åse Strandbu, "En 'sykt' seriøs ungdomsgenerasjon? [A 'sickly serious' youth generation?]", *Journal of the Norwegian Psychologist Association* 50, no. 4 (2013).
18 Kristoffer Chelsom Vogt, "Vår utålmodighet med ungdom [Our impatience with youth", *Journal of Social Research* 58, no. 1 (2017).
19 Kristoffer Chelsom Vogt, "Korsiktighetens pris [The price of short-termism]", *Journal of Social Research* 61, no. 1 (2020): 81.
20 Elisabet Christensen, "Pulver og pille [Powder and pill]", *Dagbladet* (1958, 22.2).
21 Donald Fagen, "I.G.Y. (What a beautiful world)", in *The Nightfly* (Los Angeles: Warner Bros, 1982).
22 VG, "Stadig altfor små tilførsler til Morsmelksentralen i Oslo [Constant lack of supply for the Breast Milk Centre in Oslo]", *VG* (1963, 24.7), 8.
23 Nationen, "Hva var det jeg sa? [What did I say?]" (1963, 27.12).
24 *Lofotposten*, "Stress og press [Stress and pressure]" (1968, 2.12), 7.
25 Ibid.
26 Ordnett.no, "Stress [Stress]" (2020), www.ordnett.no/search?language=no&phrase =stress.
27 Gunn Gravdal, "Stress på moten [Stress in fashion]", *Aftenposten* (1997, 13.12), 29.
28 Dana Becker, *One Nation under Stress: The Trouble with Stress as an Idea* (New York: Oxford University Press, 2013).
29 Ibid., 3.
30 Charles Taylor, *The Ethics of Authenticity* (Cambridge, MA: Harvard University Press, 1991).
31 Ole Jacob Madsen, "Drikkepress. Karakterpress. Pakkepress. Kroppspress. Stadig nye pressord, og det sier noe om oss [Drinking pressure, grade pressure, packing pressure, body pressure, constant new words for stress and that says something about us]", *Aftenposten* (2019, 2.12.), www.aftenposten.no/viten/i/pLOVaV/drikke-press-karakterpress-pakkepress-kroppspress-stadig-nye-pressord-og-det-sier-noe-om-oss-ole-jacob-madsen.

32 Queen and David Bowie, "Under pressure" (London: EMI, 1981).
33 Bakken, *Ungdata 2019. Nasjonale resultater* [*Ungdata 2019: National Results*].
34 Håkon Avseth, "Fra prestasjon til depresjon [From achievement to depression]", *NRK Ytring* (2015, 21.5), www.nrk.no/ytring/fra-prestasjon-til-depresjon-1.12369440., sec. 9.
35 Taylor, *The Ethics of Authenticity*, 40–1.
36 Ole Jacob Madsen, *Deconstructing Scandinavia's "Achievement Generation": A Youth Mental Health Crisis?*
37 Mira Aaboen Sletten, "Psykiske plager blant ungdom – og hva ungdom selv tror er årsaken [Mental health problems among adolescents – and what adolescents themselves think is the cause]", *Children in Norway* (2015).
38 Norwegian Institute of Public Health, *Psykisk helse i Norge* [*Mental Health in Norway*] (Oslo: Norwegian Institute of Public Health, 2018).
39 Beck, *Risk Society: Towards a New Modernity*, 21.
40 Christine K. Johnson et al., "Global shifts in mammalian population trends reveal key predictors of virus spillover risk", *Proceedings of the Royal Society B: Biological Sciences* 287, no. 1924 (2020).
41 NOU 2015:8, *Fremtidens skole: Fornyelse av fag og kompetanser* [*The School of the Future: Renewal of Subjects and Skills*], 19–20.
42 Katariina Mertanen, Karen Pashby, and Kristiina Brunila, "Governing young people 'at risk' with the alliance of employability and precariousness in the EU youth policy steering", *Policy Futures in Education* 18, no. 2 (2020).
43 Ibid., 255.
44 Halstensen, "Fokuset på unge menneskers psykiske helse kan være konstruktivt [The focus on young people's mental health can be constructive]", sec. 7.
45 Reidun Follesø, "Youth at risk or terms at risk?", *YOUNG* 23, no. 3 (2015).
46 Kitty te Riele, "Youth 'at risk': Further marginalizing the marginalized?", *Journal of Education Policy* 21, no. 2 (2006).
47 Karen Rebecca Foster and Dale Spencer, "At risk of what? Possibilities over probabilities in the study of young lives", *Journal of Youth Studies* 14, no. 1 (2011).
48 The Change Factory, *Timen LIVET – elevers forslag til livsmestring* [*The LIFE Hour: Student Proposals for Life Mastery*], 10.
49 Mina Gerhardsen, "Når kunnskap får skylda for samfunnsproblemer [When knowledge is blamed for social *problems*]", *Dagens Medisin* (2020, 2.3), www.dagensmedisin.no/blogger/mina-gerhardsen/2020/03/02/nar-kunnskapen-far-skylda-for-samfunnsproblemer/.
50 Samdal et al., *Stress og mestring* [*Stress and Coping*].
51 Bakken, *Ungdata 2019. Nasjonale resultater* [*Ungdata 2019: National Results*].
52 Vigdis Alver and Martin Minken, "Karakterbasert opptak: -Fører til økt segregering [Character-based admission: Leads to increased segregation]", *The Education Association* (2020, 21.1), www.utdanningsforbundet.no/nyheter/2020/karakterbasert-opptak-forer-til-okt-segregering/.
53 Richard S. Lazarus og Susan Folkman, *Stress, Appraisal and Coping* (New York: Springer, 1984).
54 Ibid., 234.
55 Ingunn Marie Eriksen et al., *Stress og press blant unge* [*Stress and Pressure among Young People*], Report no. 6/17 (Oslo: NOVA, 2017).
56 Dag Leonardsen, *Forebyggingens historie – en fortelling om et bevegelig mål* [*History of Prevention: A Tale of a Moving Target*] (Oslo: Novus, 2015), 21.
57 Gro Harlem Brundtland, "Statsministerens nyttårstale [Prime minister's new year's speech]", *NRK TV* (1992), https://tv.nrk.no/serie/statsministerens-nyttaarstale/FAKN70000191/01-01-1992, 10:30.
58 NOU 2015:8, *Fremtidens skole: Fornyelse av fag og kompetanser* [*The School of the Future: Renewal of Subjects and Skills*].

80　*Between risk and resilience*

59　Nikolas Rose, *Inventing Our Selves: Psychology, Power and Personhood* (Cambridge: Cambridge University Press, 1996).

60　Bjørnar Olsen, "En taus opposisjon [A silent opposition]", *Journal of the Norwegian Psychological Association* 52, no. 8 (2015): 641.

61　Ibid.

62　Ibid.

63　NRK District News Østfold, "Vil forebygge depresjon blant unge" [Will prevent depression among young people]" (2019, 4.10), 02:22.

64　Ibid., 02:39.

65　Norwegian Association for Cognitive Therapy, "Psykologisk førsthjelp i skolen [Psychological first aid in school]", *Norwegian Association for Cognitive Therapy* (2018, 19.4), www.kognitiv.no/psykologisk-forstehjelp-i-skolen/, sec. 2.

66　Ingebjørg Myrstad-Nilsen, "Grønne tanker-glade barn! Green thoughts-happy children!" (2017, 22.3), www.ringsaker.kommune.no/groenne-tanker-glade-barn.5974421-196585.html.

67　Ibid.

68　Daniel David, Ioana Cristea, and Stefan G. Hofmann, "Why cognitive behavioral therapy is the current gold standard of psychotherapy", *Frontiers in Psychiatry* 9, no. 4 (2018).

69　Maren Næss Olsen, "Penger, makt og menneskesyn [Money, power and human vision]", *Morgenbladet* (2012, 22.3), https://morgenbladet.no/samfunn/2012/penger_makt_og_menneskesyn.

70　Oliver Burkeman, "Therapy wars: The revenge of Freud", *The Guardian* (2016, 7.1), www.theguardian.com/science/2016/jan/07/therapy-wars-revenge-of-freud-cognitive-behavioural-therapy.

71　Torkil Berge and Arne Repål, *Den indre samtalen: Lær deg kognitiv terapi [The Inner Dialogue: Learn Cognitive Therapy]* (Oslo: Gyldendal Akademisk, 2010), 10.

72　Isaac Prilleltensky, "On the social and political implications of cognitive psychology", *The Journal of Mind and Behavior* 11, no. 2 (1990): 134.

73　Bernard Guerin, *How to Rethink Mental Illness: The Human Contexts Behind the Labels* (London: Routledge, 2017), 1.

74　NRK, "The Man", *Innafor* (2019, 20.11), 14:46.

75　Ibid., 52:23.

76　Jan Reidar Stiegler, Aksel Inge Sinding, and Leslie Greenberg, *Klok på følelser [Emotional Smarts]* (Oslo: Gyldendal Akademisk, 2018).

77　Arne Holte et al., "Ny lærerplan i skolen uten psykisk helse? Dette kan du ikke leve med, Sanner [New curriculum in schools without mental health? You can't live like this, Sanner]".

78　Aristotle, *Rhetoric* (Mineola, NY: Dover, 2012).

79　See Stiegler, Sinding, and Greenberg, *Klok på følelser [Emotional Smarts]*; Arne Holte, "Sats bredt på psykisk helse i barnehagen og skolen! [Focus broadly on mental health in kindergarten and school!]", *Psykologisk.no* (2016, 18.6), https://psykologisk.no/2016/06/sats-bredt-pa-psykisk-helse-i-barnehage-og-skole/.

80　The Norwegian Psychological Association et al., *Boken som mangler [The Book That Is Missing]*.

81　Tor Levin Hofgaard, "Psykologi må bli pensum! [Psychology must become the syllabus!]", *NRK Ytring* (2015), www.nrk.no/ytring/psykologi-ma-bli-pensum_-1.12499881, sec. 3.

82　Ibid., sec. 6.

83　Ibid., sec. 4.

84　The Storting, "Stortinget – Møte tirsdag den 12. april 2016 kl. 10 [The storting: Meeting on Tuesday, 12 April 2016 at 10]."

85　Solfrid Raknes, *Psykologisk førstehjelp barn [Psychological First Aid Children]* (Oslo: Gyldendal Academic, 2010); *Psykologisk førstehjelp ungdom [Psychological First Aid Youth]* (Oslo: Gyldendal Akademisk, 2010).

86 Camilla Lauritzen, "Alle har en psykisk helse [Everyone has a mental health]", *Ungsinn* (2012, 5.6), https://ungsinn.no/post_tiltak/alle-har-en-psykisk-helse/.

87 Ida Brandtzæg, Stig Torsteinson, and Guro Øiestad, "Folkehelse og livsmestring i skolen [Health and life skills in school]", *Journal of the Norwegian Psychologist Association* 54, no. 8 (2017): 766.

88 Ingrid Lund, "Relasjonskompetanse inn i lærerutdanningen [Relational competence into teacher education]", *Better School*, no. 1 (2017), https://utdanningsforskning.no/artikler/relasjonskompetanse-inn-i-larerutdanningene/.

89 The Norwegian Directorate of Health, "Tiltak i program for folkehelsearbeid i kommunene [Measures in programmes for public health work in the municipalities]", *forebygging.no* (2020), http://handling.forebygging.no/folkehelsearbeid/.

90 Jogeir Sognæs, "Psykologer kan motvirke at skolen skaper tapere [Psychologists can prevent the school from creating losers]", *Journal of the Norwegian Psychologist Association* 41, no. 12 (2004).

91 Jørg Arne Jørgensen, "Søkelyset på 'presset og stresset' hos unge [The spotlight on the "pressure and stress" in young people]", *Stavanger Aftenblad* (2019, 12.10), www.aftenbladet.no/meninger/kommentar/i/9v0raq/skelyset-pa-presset-og-stresset-hos-unge.

92 Ibid., sec. 12.

93 Lars Johan Masterstvedt, "Selvbestemmelssretten – en hellig ku i det sekulære Vesten [The right of self-determination: A sacred cow in the secular West]", *New Norwegian Journal* 36, no. 3 (2019): 230.

94 Roy Baumeister, "The self and society: Changes, problems, and opportunities", in *Self and Identity*, ed. Richard D. Ashmore and Lee Jussim (New York: Oxford University Press, 1997), 214.

95 Ole Jacob Madsen and Brita Ytre-Arne, "Me at my best: Therapeutic ideals in Norwegian women's magazines", *Communication, Culture and Critique* 5, no. 1 (2012).

96 Gjyri Helén Werp, "Meg på mitt beste [Me at my best]", *Kvinner & Klær* (2010, 16.7).

97 Ole Jacob Madsen, *Optimizing the Self* (London: Routledge, 2015).

98 Madsen, *The Therapeutic Turn*.

100 Ibid., sec. 3.

101 Sindre Murtnes, "Golfstjerner ser til mentale trenere – Hovland er skeptisk [Golf stars look to mental coaches: Hovland is skeptical]", *NRK* (2020, 26.2), www.nrk.no/sport/golfstjerner-ser-til-mentale-trenere-_-hovland-er-skeptisk-1.14920047, sec. 17.

102 Meeting at the Student Community in Bergen in 1998 in connection with the 40th anniversary of the Skirbekk book *Nihilisme? Eit ungt menneskes forsøk på å orientere seg* [*Nihilism? A Young Person's Attempt to Orient Themselves*].

103 Ingeborg Misje, "Stoisk ro i hektisk tid [Stoic calm in hectic time]", *Vårt Land* (2018, 24.1), www.vl.no/nyhet/stoisk-ro-i-hektisk-tid-1.1089291?paywall=true.

104 See inter alia, Philip Rieff, *The Triumph of the Therapeutic: Uses of Faith after Freud* (Chicago, IL: University of Chicago Press, 1966); Christopher Lasch, *The Culture of Narcissism: American Life in an Age of Diminishing Expectations* (New York: Norton, 1979).

References

Aakvaag, Gunnar C. "Inger slipper unna psykologi, men det er lov å prøve [No one escapes psychology, but you're allowed to try]." *Morgenbladet* (2019, 29.11.). https://morgenbladet.no/ideer/2019/11/ingen-slipper-unna-psykologien-men-det-er-lov-prove-skriver-gunnar-c-aakvaag.

Alver, Vigdis and Martin Minken. "Karakterbasert opptak: Fører til økt segreing [Grade-based admission: Leads to increased segregation]." *Utdanningsforbundet* (2020, 21.1.). www.utdanningsforbundet.no/nyheter/2020/karakterbasert-opptak – forer-til-okt-segregering/.

Aristotle. *Rhetoric*. Mineola, NY: Dover, 2012.

Avseth, Håkon. "Fra prestasjon til depresjon [From achievement to depression]." *NRK Ytring* (2015, 21.5.). www.nrk.no/ytring/fra-prestasjon-til-depresjon-1.12369440.

Bakken, Anders. *Ungdata 2019. Nasjonale resultater [Ungdata 2019: National Results]*. NOVA Report 9/19. Oslo: NOVA, OsloMet, 2019.

Baumeister, Roy. "The self and society: Changes, problems and opportunities." In *Self and Identity*, edited by Richard D. Ashmore and Lee Jussim, 191–217. New York: Oxford University Press, 1997.

Baumeister, Roy F. and John Tierney. *Willpower: Rediscovering the Greatest Human Strength*. New York: Penguin Press, 2011.

Beck, Ulrich. *Risk Society: Towards a New Modernity*. London: Sage, 1992.

Becker, Dana. *One Nation Under Stress: The Trouble with Stress as an Idea*. New York: Oxford University Press, 2013.

Bennett, Drake. "What does the Marshmallow Test actually test?" *Bloomsberg Businessweek* (2012, 27.6.). www.bloomberg.com/bw/articles/2012-10-17/what-does-the-marshmallow-test-actually-test.

Berge, Torkil and Arne Repål. *Den indre samtalen: Lær deg kognitiv terapi [The Inner Dialogue: Learn Cognitive Therapy]*. Oslo: Gyldendal Akademisk, 2010.

Bernard Guerin. *How to Rethink Mental Illness: The Human Contexts behind the Labels*. London: Routledge, 2017.

The Bible. *The Bible: Authorized King James Version*. Oxford: Oxford University Press, 2008.

Brandtzæg, Ida, Stig Torsteinson and Guro Øiestad. "Folkehelse og livsmestring i skolen [Health and life skills in school]." *Journal of the Norwegian Psychological Association* 54, no. 8 (2017): 766–7).

Brinkmann, Svend, Anders Petersen, Ester Holte Kofod and Rasmus Birk. "Diagnosekultur – et analytisk perspektiv på psykiatriske diagnoser i samtiden [Diagnosis culture: An analytical perspective on contemporary psychiatric diagnoses]." *Journal of the Norwegian Psychological Association* 51, no. 9 (2014): 692–7.

Brundtland, Gro Harlem. "Statsministerens nyttårstale [The Prime Minister's New Year speech]." *NRK TV* (1992). https://tv.nrk.no/serie/statsministerens-nyttaarstale/FAKN70000191/01-01-1992.

Burkeman, Oliver. "Therapy wars: The revenge of Freud." *The Guardian* (2016, 7.1.). www.theguardian.com/science/2016/jan/07/therapy-wars-revenge-of-freud-cognitive-behavioural-therapy.

Carney, Dana R., Amy J.C. Cuddy and Andy J. Yap. "Power posing: Brief nonverbal displays affect neuroendocrine levels and risk tolerance." *Psychological Science* 21, no. 10 (2010): 1363–8.

Charlton, Bruce G. "A critique of Geoffrey Rose's 'population strategy' for preventive medicine." *Journal of the Royal Society of Medicine* 88, no. 11 (1995): 607–10.

Christensen, Elisabet. "Pulver og pille [Powder and pill]." *Dagbladet* 3 (1958, 22.2).

Christensen, Lina. "Forskernes politiske fortrinn [The political advantage of the researchers]." *Forskerforum* 52, no. 4 (2020): 19–23.

Crawford, Robert. "Healthism and the medicalisation of everyday life." *International Journal of Health Services* 10, no. 3 (1980): 365–88.

Cuddy, Amy. "Your body language may shape who you are." *TED* (2012). www.ted.com/talks/amy_cuddy_your_body_language_may_shape_who_you_are.

Cuddy, Amy J.C., S. Jack Schultz and Nathan E. Fosse. "P-Curving a more comprehensive body of research on postural feedback reveals clear evidential value for power-posing effects." *Psychological Science* 29, no. 4 (2018): 656–66.

Dahle, Margunn Serigstad. "'Sykt perfekt' speglar presset [Sick perfect' mirrors the pressure]." *Vårt Land* (2016, 13.1.). www.vl.no/sykt-perfekt-speglar-presset-1.674304?paywall=true.

Dalrymple, Theodore. *Admirable Evasions: How Psychology Undermines Morality.* New York: Encounter Books, 2015.

David, Daniel, Ioana Cristea and Stefan G. Hofmann. "Why cognitive behavioural therapy is the current gold standard of psychotherapy." *Frontiers in Psychiatry* 9, no. 4 (2018).

Dilthey, Wilhelm. "Avgrensning av åndsvitenskapene [Delineation of intellectual science]." In *Hermeneutisk lesebok [Hermenutic Reading Book]*, edited by Sissel Lægreid and Torgeir Skogen, 215–23. Oslo: Scandinavian Academic Press, 2014.

Drugli, May Britt and Ratib Lekhal. *Livsmestring og psykisk helse [Life Mastery and Mental Health].* Oslo: Cappelen Damm Akademisk, 2018.

Ebeltoft, Joakim and Vilde Vollestad. *Undervisningsmanual. Psykologistudentes opplysningsarbeid for unge [Teaching Manual: Psychology Students' Informative Education Work for Youth].* 4th ed. Oslo: Psychology Students' Informative Education Work for Youth, 2019.

Ecclestone, Kathryn and Dennis Hayes. *The Dangerous Rise of Therapeutic Education.* London: Routledge, 2008.

Elliott, Anthony and Charles Lemert. *The New Individualism: The Emotional Costs of Globalization.* Rev. ed. New York: Routledge, 2009.

Eriksen, Ingunn Marie, Mira Aaboen Sletten, Anders Bakken and Tilmann von Soest. *Stress og press blant unge. Rapport nr. 6/17 [Stress and Pressure among Young People: Report No. 6/17].* Oslo: NOVA, 2017.

Erstad, Emil André. "KrFU vil ta oppgjør med prestasjonssamfunnet [The Christian Democratic Party will take action against the achievement society]." *Ny Tid* (2015, 5.5.). www.nytid.no/krfu-vil-ta-oppgjor-med-prestasjonssamfunnet-2/.

Fagen, Donald. "I.G.Y. (What a beautiful world)." In *The Nightfly.* Los Angeles: Warner Bros, 1982.

Fasting, Merete Lund. "Bevegelse, lek og friluftsliv kan bidra til livsmestring [Movement, play and the outdoors can contribute to life mastery]." *Utdanningsnytt* (2020, 18.3.). www.utdanningsnytt.no/livsmestring-merete-lund-fasting-utelek/bevegelse-lek-og-friluftsliv-kan-bidra-til-livsmestring/235397.

Flavell, John H. "Metacognition and cognitive monitoring: A new area of cognitive-developmental inquiry." *American Psychologist* 34, no. 10 (1979): 906–11.

Norwegian Institute of Public Health. *Psykisk helse i Norge [Mental Health in Norway].* Oslo: Norwegian Institute of Public Health, 2018.

Follesø, Reidun. "Youth at risk or terms at risk?" *Young* 23, no. 3 (2015): 240–53.

Forandringsfabrikken. *Timen LIVET – elvers forslag til livsmestring [The LIFE Hour: Student Proposals for Life Mastery].* Oslo: Forandringsfabrikken, 2019.

Foster, Karen Rebecca and Dale Spencer. "At risk of what? Possibilities over probabilities in the study of young lives." *Journal of Youth Studies* 14, no. 1 (2011): 125–43.

Foucault, Michel. *Security, Territory, Population: Lectures at the Collège de France, 1977–78.* Translated by Graham Burchell. Basingstoke: Palgrave Macmillan, 2007.

Fox, Claire. *'I Find That Offensive!'* London: Biteback, 2016.

Frohlich, Katherine L. and Louise Potvin. "Transcending the known in public health practice." *American Journal of Public Health* 98, no. 2 (2008): 216–21.

Gerhardsen, Mina. "Når kunnskapen får skylda for samfunnsproblemer [When knowledge is blamed for social problems]." *Dagens Medisin* (2020, 2.3.). www.dagensmedisin.no/blogger/mina-gerhardsen/2020/03/02/nar-kunnskapen-far-skylda-for-samfunnsproblemer/.

Glorvingen, Merete. "LisaMariaHariedestøffehøst[ThetoughfallofLisaMariaHareide]." *Kvinner & Klær* (2019). www.kk.no/livet/lisa-maria-hareides-toffe-host/70491258.

Goleman, Daniel. *Emotional Intelligence: Why It Can Matter More Than IQ.* London: Bloomsbury, 1996.

Gravdal, Gunn. "Stress på moten [Stress is in fashion]." *Aftenposten* (1997, 13.12): 29.

Halstensen, Kari. "Fokuset på unge menneskers psykiske helse kan være konstruktivt [The focus on young people's mental health can be constructive]." *Aftenposten* (2020, 11.2.). www.aftenposten.no/meninger/debatt/i/naKA7B/fokuset-paa-unge-menneskers-psykiske-helse-kan-vaere-konstruktivt-kari-halstensen.

Halvorsen, Joar Øveraas and Jan-Ole Hesselberg. "Gir pseudovitenskap på timeplanen bedre livsmestring? [Does pseudoscience on the schedule improve life mastery?]" *Aftenposten* (2019, 28.4.). www.aftenposten.no/meninger/debatt/i/VbgvJ4/gir-pseudovitenskap-paa-timeplanen-bedre-livsmestring-halvorsen-og-hesselberg?

Halvorsen, Kristin and Irene L. Lystrup. "Kronprinsparets Fond svarer på kritikken: De unge lærer mange ulike strategier for å mestre livet bedre [The Crown Prince's Fund responds to the criticism: Young people learn many different strategies to cope with life better]." *Aftenposten* (2019, 15.10.). www.aftenposten.no/meninger/debatt/i/GG88Mx/kronprinsparets-fond-svarer-paa-kritikken-de-unge-laerer-mange-ulike-strategier-for-aa-mestre-livet-bedre-kristin-halvorsen-og-irene-l-lystrup.

Halvorsen, Per. "-Ikke fred uten psykologi [-No peace without psychology]." *Norwegian Psychological Association* (2011, 6.9.). http://psykologforeningen.no/Foreningen/Nyheter-og-aktuelt/Aktuelt/Ikke-fred-uten-psykologi/%28language%29/nor-NO.

———. "Tilpasser utdanningen til nye psykologroller [Adapting education to new psychologist roles]." *Norwegian Psychological Association* (2019, 28.2.). www.psykologforeningen.no/foreningen/aktuelt/aktuelt/tilpasser-utdanningen-til-nye-psykologroller.

Hansen, Jonathan Simchai. "Viktor Hovlands vei til toppen [Viktor Hovland's road to the top]." *VG* (2020, 6.3.). www.vg.no/sport/i/6j0QMr/viktor-hovlands-vei-til-toppen.

Hegna, Kristinn, Guro Ødegård and Åse Strandbu. "En 'sykt' seriøs ungdomsgenerasjon? [A 'seriously sick' youth generation?]" *Journal of the Norwegian Psychological Association* 50, no. 4 (2013): 374–77.

Hobbelstad, Inger Merete. "Neste gang du hører Høyre-folk snake om å verne norsk kultur, må du le. På deres vakt skamferes norskfaget [The next time you hear the Conservatives talking about protecting Norwegian culture, you have to laugh: On their watch, the subject of Norwegian is mutilated]." *Dagbladet* (2018, 25.3.). www.dagbladet.no/kultur/neste-gang-du-horer-hoyre-folk-snakke-om-a-verne-norsk-kultur-ma-du-le-pa-deres-vakt-skamferes-norskfaget/69582172.

Hofgaard, Tor Levin. "Psykologi må bli pensum! [Psychology must become the syllabus!]" *NRK Ytring* (2015, 17.8.). www.nrk.no/ytring/psykologi-ma-bli-pensum_-1.12499881.

Høihjelle, Mari Valen. "Joda, du greier å stå imot fristelsene [Sure, you can resist temptation]." *ABC Nyheter* (2013, 9.6.). www.abcnyheter.no/livet/2013/06/09/175021/joda-du-greier-sta-imot-fristelsene.

Holte, Arne. "Sats bredt på psykisk helse i barnehagen og skolen! [Focus broadly on mental health in kindergarten and school!]" *Psykologisk.no* (2016, 18.6.). https://psykologisk.no/2016/06/sats-bredt-pa-psykisk-helse-i-barnehage-og-skole/.

———. "Slik fremmer vi psykisk helse, forebygger psykiske lidelser og får en mer fornuftig samfunnsøkonomi [How we promote mental health, prevent psychological disorders and get more sensible social economics]." *Utposten: Academic Magazine for General and Public Medicine* no. 2 (2017). www.utposten.no/i/2017/2/utposten-2-2017b-457.

———. "Forebygging av depressive plager hos barn og unge – på tvers av arenaer [Prevention of depressive problems in children and adolescents: Across arenas]." *Psykologisk.no* (2019, 23.4.). https://psykologisk.no/2019/04/forebygging-av-depressive-plager-hos-barn-og-unge-pa-tvers-av-arenaer/.

Holte, Arne, Hilde Aarflot, Nina Grindheim, Espen Hansen, Anne Torhild Klomsten, Egil Nygaard and Veronica Pedersen. "Ny lærerplan i skolen uten psykisk helse? Dette kan du ikke leve med, Sanner [New curriculum in schools without mental health? You can't live like this, Sanner]." *Aftenposten* (2019, 12.5.). www.aftenposten.no/meninger/kronikk/i/GGwvGl/ny-laereplan-i-skolen-uten-psykisk-helse-dette-kan-du-ikke-leve-med-sanner.

Holterman, Sonja and Kari Oliv Vedvik. "-Elever har følt seg presset til å dele ting med klassen [-Students have felt pressured to share things with the class]." *Utdanningsnytt* (2020, 15.3.). www.utdanningsnytt.no/fagfornyelsen-livsmestring/foreldre-reagerer – elever-har-folt-seg-presset-til-a-dele-ting-med-klassen/234166.

Jakobsen, Siw Ellen. "Selvregulering er grunnmuren for læring [Self-regulation is the foundation for learning]." *forskning.no* (2015, 25.1.). http://forskning.no/barn-og-ungdom-psykologi/2015/01/selvregulering-er-grunnmuren-laering.

Johnson, Christine K., Peta L. Hitchens, Pranav S. Pandit, Julie Rushmore, Tierra Smiley Evans, Cristin C.W. Young and Megan M. Doyle. "Global shifts in mammalian population trends reveal key predictors of virus spillover risk." *Proceedings of the Royal Society B: Biological Sciences* 287, no. 1924 (2020): 20192736.

Johnson, Sverre Urnes, Ragnfrid Nordbø, Jone Solberg Vik, Ingunn Herfinda, Ivar Ødegård, Mette Skikstein and Hanne Mjølid Braathen. "Psykisk helse i skolen: #psyktnormalt [School mental health: #psychnormal]." *Utdanningsnytt* (2019, 25.7.). www.utdanningsnytt.no/psykisk-helse/psykisk-helse-i-skolen-psyktnormalt/206298.

Jørgensen, Jørg Arne. "Søkelyset på 'presset og stresset' hos unge [The spotlight on 'pressure and stress' of young people]." *Stavanger Aftenblad* (2019, 12.10.). www.aftenbladet.no/meninger/kommentar/i/9v0raq/skelyset-pa-presset-og-stresset-hos-unge.

Kaurel, Jon. *Tidlig innsats i utdanningspolitikken – motive, mål og motsetninger [Early Intervention in Education Policy: Motives, Goals and Contradictions]*. Oslo: Utdanningsforbundet, 2018.

Keay, Douglas. "Interview for *Woman's Own* ('No such thing as society')." (1987). www.margaretthatcher.org/document/106689.

Kidd, Celeste, Holly Palmeri and Richard N. Aslin. "Rational snacking: Young children's decision-making on the marshmallow task is moderated by beliefs about environmental reliability." *Cognition* 126, no. 1 (2013): 109–14.

Klomsten, Anne Torhild. *Livsmestring på timeplanen: Utdanning I PSykisk helse [Life Mastery on the Schedule: Education in Mental Health]*. Trondheim: NTNU, 2018.

Kommandantvold, Maria and Ida Gjellerud. "Slik skal ungdommen lære å mestre hverdagen [How young people will learn to cope with everyday life]." *NRK* (2019,24.4.). www. nrk.no/osloogviken/slik-skal-ungdommen-laere-a-mestre-hverdagen-1.14520405.

Larsen, Dag Eivind Undheim. "Pedagoger på dypt vann [Pedagogues in deep water]." *Klassekampen* (2018, 8.12.). www.klassekampen.no/article/20181208/ARTICLE/181209971.

Lasch, Christopher. *The Culture of Narcissism: American Life in an Age of Diminishing Expectations.* New York: Norton, 1979.

Lauritzen, Camilla. "Alle har en psykisk helse [Everyone has a mental health]." *Ungsinn* (2012, 5.6.). https://ungsinn.no/post_tiltak/alle-har-en-psykisk-helse/.

Lazarus, Richard S. and Susan Folkman. *Stress, Appraisal and Coping.* New York: Springer, 1984.

LeCroy, Craig Winston and Elizabeth K Anthony. "Youth at risk." *Oxford Bibliographies* (2018). www.oxfordbibliographies.com/view/document/obo-9780195389678/obo-9780195389678-0112.xml#firstMatch.

Lemke, Thomas. "The Birth of Bio-Politics: Michel Foucault's lecture at the Collège de France on neo-liberal governmentality." *Economy and Society* 30, no. 2 (2001): 190–207.

Leonardsen, Dag. *Forebyggingens historie – en fortelling om et bevegelig mål [History of Prevention: A Tale of a Moving Target].* Oslo: Novus, 2015.

Lid, Jon and Andreas Riis, Eds. *Studentene fra 1909 [The Students from 1909].* Oslo: Det Mallingske Boktrykkeri, 1959.

Livingston, Jennifer A. "Metacognition: An overview." (1997). https://eric.ed.gov/?id=ED474273.

Lofotposten. "Stress og press [Stress and pressure]." *Lofotposten,* (1968, 12.2): 7.

Løgstrup, Knud Ejler. *Den etiske fordring [The Ethical Claim].* Oslo: Cappelen, 2000.

Lund, Ingrid. "Relasjonskompetanse inn i lærerutdanningene [Relational competence into teacher education]." *Better School,* no. 1 (2017). https://utdanningsforskning.no/artikler/relasjonskompetanse-inn-i-larerutdanningene/.

The Lutheran Confessional Church. "Som sauer uten hyrde [Like sheep without a shepherd]." *The Lutheran Confessional Church* (2003). www.luthersk-kirke.no/lbk-luthersk-kirke.no/andakt17-2003.htm.

Madsen, Ole Jacob. *The Therapeutic Turn.* London: Routledge, 2014.

———. *Optimizing the Self.* London: Routledge, 2015.

———. "Den terapeutiske skolesekken? [The therapeutic schoolbag?]" In *Rapporten. Sjanger og styringsverktøy [The Report: Genre and Management Tool],* edited by Kristian Bjørkdahl, 203–29. Oslo: Pax, 2018.

———. "Drikkepress. Karakterpress. Pakkepress. Kroppspress. Stadig nye pressord, og det sier noe om oss [Drinking pressure. Grade pressure. Packing pressure. Body pressure. Constantly new words of pressure and that says something about us]." *Aftenposten* (2019, 2.12.). www.aftenposten.no/viten/i/pLOVaV/drikkepress-karakterpress-pakkepress-kroppspress-stadig-nye-pressord-og-det-sier-noe-om-oss-ole-jacob-madsen.

———. "Ingen velger å bli syke. Men kulturell påvirkning forekommer [But no one chooses to get sick: But cultural influence is present]." *Aftenposten* (2020, 11.2.). www.aftenposten.no/viten/i/Jo4oo8/ingen-velger-aa-bli-syke-men-kulturell-paavirkning-forekommer-ole-jacob-madsen?

———. *Deconstructing Scandinavia's 'Achievement Generation': A Youth Mental Health Crisis?* London: Palgrave, 2021.

Madsen, Ole Jacob and Brita Ytre-Arne. "Me at my best: Therapeutic ideals in Norwegian women's magazines." *Communication, Culture and Critique* 5, no. 1 (2012): 20–37.

Martin, Jack and Ann-Marie McLellan. *The Education of Selves: How Psychology Transformed Students.* New York: Oxford University Press, 2013.

Masterstvedt, Lars Johan. "Selvbestemmelsesretten – en hellig ku i det sekulære Vesten [The right of self-determination: A sacred cow in the secular West]." *Nytt Norsk Tidsskrift* 36, no. 3 (2019): 230–40.

Melas, Chloe. "Brad Pitt on Angelina Jolie in new court documents: 'She has no self-regulation mechanism'." *CNN* (2016, 22.12.). https://edition.cnn.com/2016/12/22/entertainment/brad-pitt-court-documents-custody/index.html.

Mertanen, Katariina, Karen Pashby and Kristiina Brunila. "Governing young people 'at risk' with the alliance of employability and precariousness in the EU youth policy steering." *Policy Futures in Education* 18, no. 2 (2020): 240–60.

Miller, George A. "Psychology as a means of promoting human welfare." *American Psychologist* 24, no. 12 (1969): 1063–75.

Mischel, Walter. "Preference for delayed reinforcement: An experimental study of a cultural observation." *The Journal of Abnormal and Social Psychology* 56, no. 1 (1958): 57–61.

Mischel, Walter, Ebbe B. Ebbesen and Antonette R. Zeiss. "Cognitive and attentional mechanisms in delay of gratification." *Journal of Personality and Social Psychology* 21, no. 2 (1972): 204–18.

Mischel, Walter, Yuichi Shoda and Philip K. Peake. "The nature of adolescent competencies predicted by preschool delay of gratification." *Journal of Personality and Social Psychology* 54, no. 4 (1988): 687–96.

Moen, Ole Martin. "Fremtidsskolen [School of the future]." *Dagbladet* (2018, 12.2.). www.dagbladet.no/kultur/fremtidsskolen/69443837.

Murtnes, Sindre. "Golfstjerner ser til mentale trenere – Hovland er skeptisk [Golf stars look to mental coaches: Hovland is skeptical]." *NRK* (2020, 26.2.). www.nrk.no/sport/golfstjerner-ser-til-mentale-trenere-_-hovland-er-skeptisk-1.14920047.

Mykkeltveit, Pål. "Det er galt å tro at konservativ politikk mister relevans i krisetider [It is wrong to think that conservative politics loses relevance in times of crisis]." *Minerva* (2020, 31.3.). www.minervanett.no/boris-johnson-konservatisme-koronavirus/det-er-galt-a-tro-at-konservativ-politikk-mister-relevans-i-krisetider/356100.

Myrstad-Nilsen, Ingebjørg. "Grønne tanker – glade barn! [Green thoughts: Happy children!]" (2017, 22.3.). www.ringsaker.kommune.no/groenne-tanker-glade-barn.5974421-196585.html.

The National Commission on Excellence in Education. *A Nation at Risk: The Imperative for Educational Reform.* Washington, DC: The National Commission on Excellence in Education, 1983.

Nationen. "Hva var det jeg sa? [What did I say?]" *Nationen* (1963, 27.12): 6.

Neumann, Iver B. and Ole Jacob Sending. "Du skal regjere deg selv [You shall regulate yourself]." *Le Monde Diplomatique, Nordic Edition* (2003): 1–2.

Nielsen, Torben Hviid. "De 'frisatte'. Om individualisering og identitet i nyere samtidsdiagnoser [The 'freed' : On individualisation and identity in recent contemporary diagnoses]." In *Klassebilder: Ulikheter og sosial mobilitet i Norge [Class Photos: Differences and Social Mobility in Norway]*, edited by Kenneth Dahlgren and Jørn Ljunggren, 169–81. Oslo: Universitetsforlaget, 2010.

Norwegian Association for Cognitive Therapy. "Psykologisk førstehjelp i skolen [Psychological first aid in school]." *Norwegian Association for Cognitive Therapy* (2018, 19.4.). www.kognitiv.no/psykologisk-forstehjelp-i-skolen/.

Norwegian Centre for Learning Environment and Behavioural Research in Education. *Robust [Robust]*. Stavanger: University of Stavanger, 2020.

The Norwegian Children and Youth Council. *Livsmestring i skolen: For flere små og store seire i hverdagen [Life Mastery in School: For Several Small and Large Victories in Everyday Life]* (2017). www.lnu.no/wp-content/uploads/2017/01/lis-sluttrapport-1.pdf.

Norwegian Directorate of Education. *Rammeplan for barnehagen [National Curriculum Regulations for Kindergarten and Daycare Facilities]*. Oslo: Norwegian Directorate of Education, 2017.

———. *Lærerplanverket [Curriculum]*. Oslo: Norwegian Directorate for Education and Training, 2020. www.udir.no/lk20/overordnet-del/prinsipper-for-laring-utvikling-og-danning/tverrfaglige-temaer/folkehelse-og-livsmestring/.

The Norwegian Directorate of Health. "Tiltak i program for folkehelsearbeid i kommunene [Measures in programmes for work in public health in the municipalities]." *forebygging.no* (2020). http://handling.forebygging.no/folkehelsearbeid/.

The Norwegian Psychological Association. "Prinsippprogram [Principles programme]." *Norwegian Psychological Association* (2010). www.psykologforeningen.no/foreningen/vedtekter-og-retningslinjer/prinsipprogram.

The Norwegian Psychological Association, the Student Organisation, Youth Mental Health, Norwegian Lector Union, the Norwegian Psychiatric Association and the Council for Mental Health. *Boken som mangler [The Book That Is Missing]* (2015). www.psykologforeningen.no/foreningen/nyheter-og-kommentarer/aktuelt/krever-psykologi-i-skolen#opprop.

NOU 2014:7. *Elevenes læring i fremtidens skole [Student Learning in the School of the Future]*, edited by Ministry of Education and Research. Oslo: The Norwegian Government Security and Service Organisation, 2014.

——— 2015:8. *Fremtidens skole [The School of the Future: Renewal of Subjects and Skills]*. Oslo: Ministry of Education and Research, 2015.

NRK. "The man." In *Innafor*, edited by NRK, https://tv.nrk.no/serie/innafor/2019/MDDP12100719/avspiller, 2019, 20.11.

NRK Distriktsnyheter Østfold. "Vil forebygge depresjon blant unge [Will prevent depression among young people]." (2019, 4.10.). https://tv.nrk.no/serie/distriktsnyheter-oestfold/201910/DKOS99100419/avspiller.

NRK P2. "Nyhetsmorgen [New morning]." (2019, 8.10.). https://radio.nrk.no/serie/nyhetsmorgen/NPUB32020019/08-10-2019.

NRK School. "Hva er psykisk helse? [What is mental health?]" *Briefly Explained: Life Mastery* (2019, 5.10). www.nrk.no/skole/?mediaId=24134&page=search&program=Kort%20fortalt%20-%20livsmestring.

———. "Hva er en tanke? [What is a thought?]" *Briefly Explained: Life Mastery* (2019, 7.10). www.nrk.no/skole/?mediaId=24132&page=search&program=Kort%20fortalt%20-%20livsmestring.

Olsen, Bjørnar. "En taus opposisjon [A silent opposition]." *Journal of the Norwegian Psychological Association* 52, no. 8 (2015): 641.

Olsen, Maren Næss. "Penger, makt og menneskesyn [Money, power and human vision]." *Morgenbladet* (2012, 22.3.). https://morgenbladet.no/samfunn/2012/penger_makt_og_menneskesyn.

Ordnett.no. "Stress" (2020). www.ordnett.no/search?language=no&phrase=stress.

Phelan, Jo C. and Bruce G. Link. "Controlling disease and creating disparities: A fundamental cause perspective." *Journals of Gerontology: SERIES B* 60B, no. Special Issue II (2005): 27–33.

Pink, Hartmut. *Fremmedgørelse og acceleration [Alienation and Acceleration]*. Copenhagen: Hans Reitzel, 2014.

Prilleltensky, Isaac. "On the social and political implications of cognitive psychology." *The Journal of Mind and Behaviour* 11, no. 2 (1990): 127–36.

Queen and David Bowie. "Under pressure." In *Single*. London: EMI, 1981.

Raknes, Solfrid. *Psykologisk førstehjelp barn [Psychological First Aid Children]*. Oslo: Gyldendal Akademisk, 2010.

———. *Psykologisk førstehjelp ungdom [Psychological First Aid Young People]*. Oslo: Gyldendal Akademisk, 2010.

Ranehill, Eva, Anna Dreber, Magnus Johannesson, Susanne Leiberg, Sunhae Sul and Roberto A. Weber. "Assessing the robustness of power posing: No effect on hormones and risk tolerance in a large sample of men and women." *Psychological Science* 26, no. 5 (2015): 653–6.

Rege, Mari. "Professor Mari Rege fra UiS på NHOs Årskonferanse 2014 [Professor Mari Rege from UiS at the NHO Annual Conference 2014]." www.youtube.com/watch?v=a6LoniVClYc, 2014.

Reite, Gunhild Nordvik. "NRKs 'Livsmestring' har bismak [NRK's 'Life Mastery' has an aftertaste]." *Dagbladet* (2019, 13.11.). www.dagbladet.no/kultur/nrks-livsmestring-har-bismak/71804799.

Report to the Storting. Report. St. 6. *Tett på – tidlig innsats og inkluderende fellesskap i barnehage, skole og SFO [Close: Early Intervention and Inclusive Communities in Kindergarten and Daycare Facilities, Schools and SFO]*. Oslo: Ministry of Education and Research. 2019–2020.

———. Report. St. 19. *Folkehelsemeldina. Gode liv i eit trygt samfunn [Public Health Report: Good Lives in a Safe Society]*. Oslo: Norwegian Ministry of Health and Care Services. 2018–2019.

———. Report. St. 19. *Folkehelsemeldingen. Mestring og muligheter [Public Health Report: Coping and Opportunities]*. Oslo: Norwegian Ministry of Health and Care Services. 2014–2015.

———. Report. St. 28. *Fag – Fordypning – Forståelse. En fornyelse av Kunnskapsløftet [Subject – Specialisation – Understanding: A Renewal of the Knowledge Promotion Reform]*. Oslo: Ministry of Education and Research. 2016.

———. Report. St. 34. *Folkehelsemeldingen. God helse – felles ansvar. [Public Health Report: Good Health: Joint Responsibility]*. Oslo: Norwegian Ministry of Health and Care Services. 2012–2013.

Rieff, Philip. *The Triumph of the Therapeutic: Uses of Faith After Freud*. Chicago, IL: University of Chicago Press, 1966.

Riele, Kitty te. "Youth 'at risk': Further marginalizing the marginalized?" *Journal of Education Policy* 21, no. 2 (2006): 129–45.

Ropstad, Kjell Ingolf. "-Ingen skal kunne si at jeg var stille da de trengte meg [-No one should be able to say that I was quiet when they needed me]." Christian Democratic Party (2019, 28.4.). www.krf.no/nyheter/nyheter-fra-krf/-ingen-skal-kunne-si-at-jeg-var-stille-da-de-trengte-meg/.

Rose, Geoffrey. "Sick individuals and sick populations." *International Journal of Epidemiology* 14 (1985): 32–8.

————. *The Strategy of Preventive Medicine*. Oxford: Oxford University Press, 1992.

Rose, Nikolas. *Inventing Our Selves: Psychology, Power and Personhood*. Cambridge: Cambridge University Press, 1996.

RVTS South. *Lærerveiledning til LINK [Teacher's Guide to LINK]*. Kristiansand: RVTS South, 2017.

Sæbjørnsen, Daniel. "Generasjon prestasjon trenger å ledes til liv [Generation achievement needs to be led to life]." *Tro & Medier* (2019, 13.11.). https://troogmedier.no/ generasjon-prestasjon-trenger-a-ledes-til-liv/.

Sælebakke, Anne. *Livsmestring i skolen. Et relasjonelt perspektiv [Life mastery in school. A relational perspective]*. Oslo: Gyldendal Akademisk, 2018.

Sælid, Gry Anette. "Tankekraft – eit livsmestringsprogram. Prosjektbeskrivelse [The power of thought: A life mastery programme. Project description]." Norwegian Institute of Public Health (2018, 20.11.). www.fhi.no/cristin-prosjekter/aktiv/ mentale-teknikker-i-hverdagen-mt/.

Samdal, Oddrun, Bente Would, Anette Harris and Torbjørn Torsheim. *Stress og mestring [Stress and Coping]*. Oslo: The Norwegian Directorate of Health, 2017.

Sanner, Jan Tore. "Elevene skal lære mer om psykisk helse og livsmestring i skolen [Students should learn more about mental health and life coping at school]." *Aftenposten* (2019, 19.5.). www.aftenposten.no/meninger/debatt/i/y3xVpR/ elevene-skal-laere-mer-om-psykisk-helse-og-livsmestring-i-skolen-jan-tore-sanner.

Skre, Ingunn B. "Resiliens [Resilience]." *Store norske leksikon* (2019). https://snl.no/ resiliens.

Skregelid, Lisbet. "Generasjon prestasjon og kunsten å mestre livet [Generation achievement and the art of coping with life]." University of Agder (2018, 18.10.). www.uia.no/nyheter/generasjon-prestasjon-og-kunsten-aa-mestre-livet.

Sletten, Mira Aaboen. "Psykiske plager blant Ungdom – og hva ungdom selv tror er årsaken [Mental health problems among adolescents: And what adolescents themselves think is the cause]." *Children in Norway* (2015): 8–25.

Sognæs, Jogeir. "Psykologer kan motvirke at skolen skaper tapere [Psychologists can discourage schools from creating losers]." *Journal of the Norwegian Psychological Association* 41, no. 12 (2004): 1019–20.

Stiegler, Jan Reidar, Aksel Inge Sinding and Leslie Greenberg. *Klok på følelser [Emotional Smarts]*. Oslo: Gyldendal Akademisk, 2018.

Stockings, Emily, Louisa Degenhardt, Timothy Dobbins, Yong Lee, Holly Erskine, Harvey Whiteford and George Patton. "Preventing depression and anxiety in young people: A review of the joint efficacy of universal, selective and indicated prevention." *Psychological Medicine* 46, no. 1 (2016): 11–26.

The Storting. "Stortinget – Møte tirsdag den 12. april 2016 kl. 10 [The Storting: Meeting on Tuesday, 12 April 2016 at 10]" (2016, 12.4.). www.stortinget.no/nn/Saker-og-publikasjonar/publikasjonar/Referat/Stortinget/2015-2016/160412/5/., 4:27:02.

Svartdal, Frode. "Selvregulering [Self-regulation]." *Store norske leksikon* (2014). https://snl.no/selvregulering.

————. "Mestring [Coping]." *Store norske leksikon* (2018). https://snl.no/mestring.

Taylor, Charles. *The Ethics of Authenticity*. Cambridge, MA: Harvard University Press, 1991.

Telhaug, Alfred Oftedal. *Grunnskolen som nasjonsbygger [Primary School and Lower Secondary School as a Nation Builder]*. Oslo: Abstrakt forlag, 2003, 415.

Utdanningsnytt. "Rapport: 13 åringer bør få undervisning i livsmestring [Report: 13-year-olds should be taught life mastery]." *Utdanningsnytt* (2017, 24.1.). www. utdanningsnytt.no/rapport-13-aringer-bor-fa-undervisning-i-livsmestring/180235.

VG. "Stadig altfor små tilførsler til Morsmelksentralen i Oslo [Constant lack of supply for the Breast Milk Centre in Oslo]." *VG*, (1963, 24.7): 8.

Vibe, Ingeborg "Stoisk ro i hektisk tid [Stoic calm in hectic times]." *Vårt Land* (2018, 24.1.). www.vl.no/nyhet/stoisk-ro-i-hektisk-tid-1.1089291?paywall=true.

Vik, Stine. "Tidlig innsats og barnehagen som forebyggingsarena [Early intervention and kindergarten as a prevention arena]." In *Kindergarten as a Community Institution*, edited by Solveig Østrem, 143–58. Oslo: Cappelen Akademisk, 2018.

Visjø, Camilla Tryggestad and Nils Bjåland. "Klarer barnet ditt å motstå denne? [Can your child resist this?]" *VG* (2013, 1.11.). www.vg.no/nyheter/innenriks/i/L0x1J4/klarer-barnet-ditt-aa-motstaa-denne.

Vogt, Kristoffer Chelsom. "Vår utålmodighet med ungdom [Our impatience with youth]." *Journal of Social Research* 58, no. 1 (2017): 105–19.

———. "Kortsiktighetens pris [The price of short-termism]." *Journal of Social Research* 61, no. 1 (2020): 80–2.

Watts, Tyler W., Greg J. Duncan and Haonan Quan. "Revisiting the marshmallow test: A conceptual replication investigating links between early delay of gratification and later outcomes." *Psychological Science* 29, no. 7 (2018): 1159–77.

Weare, Katherine and Melanie Nind. "Mental health promotion and problem prevention in schools: What does the evidence say?" *Health Promotion International* 26, no. suppl_1 (2011): i29–i69.

Werner-Seidler, Aliza, Yael Perry, Alison L. Calear, Jill M. Newby and Helen Christensen. "School-based depression and anxiety prevention programs for young people: A systematic review and meta-analysis." *Clinical Psychology Review* 51 (2017): 30–47.

Werp, Gjyri Helén. "Meg på mitt beste [Me at my best]." *Kvinner & Klær*, (2010, 16.7): 5.

WHO. *Growing Up Unequal: Gender and Socioeconomic Differences in Young People's Health and Well-being.* Copenhagen: WHO, 2016.

———. "Constitution." (2020). www.who.int/about/who-we-are/constitution.

Wood, Joanne V., W.Q. Perunovic and John W. Lee. "Positive self-statements." *Psychological Science* 20, no. 7 (2009): 860–6.

World Economic Forum. *New Vision for Education.* Geneva: World Economic Forum, 2015.

Yousefi, Shaghayegh " – Det forventes mer av oss på alle arenaer [-More is expected of us in all arenas]." *Aftenposten*, (2017, 10.7): 6–7.

Index

For Product Safety Concerns and Information please contact our EU
representative GPSR@taylorandfrancis.com
Taylor & Francis Verlag GmbH, Kaufingerstraße 24, 80331 München, Germany

www.ingramcontent.com/pod-product-compliance
Lightning Source LLC
Chambersburg PA
CBHW071053280326
41928CB00050B/2500